Family &

Cookbook

From Casserole Suppers
to Champagne Celebrations,
50 Menus, Meal Plans,
and More Than
200 Healthy Recipes
for Every Occasion

A Healthy Exchanges® Cookbook

JoAnna M. Lund

With Barbara Alpert

A Perigee Book

A Perigee Book
Published by the Penguin Group
Penguin Group (USA) Inc.
375 Hudson Street, New York, New York 10014, USA
Penguin Group (Canada), 10 Alcorn Avenue, Toronto, Ontario M4V 3B2, Canada
(a division of Pearson Penguin Canada Inc.)
Penguin Books Ltd., 80 Strand, London WC2R 0RL, England
Penguin Group Ireland, 25 St. Stephen's Green, Dublin 2, Ireland (a division of Penguin Books Ltd.)
Penguin Group (Australia), 250 Camberwell Road, Camberwell, Victoria 3124, Australia
(a division of Pearson Australia Group Pty. Ltd.)
Penguin Books India Pvt. Ltd., 11 Community Centre, Panchsheel Park, New Delhi—110 017, India
Penguin Group (NZ), Cnr. Airborne and Rosedale Roads, Albany, Auckland 1310, New Zealand
(a division of Pearson New Zealand Ltd.)
Penguin Books (South Africa) (Pty.) Ltd., 24 Sturdee Avenue, Rosebank, Johannesburg 2196, South Africa
Penguin Books Ltd., Registered Offices: 80 Strand, London WC2R 0RL, England

Before using the recipes and advice in this book, consult your physician or health-care provider to be sure they are appropriate for you. The information in this book is not intended to take the place of any medical advice. It reflects the author's experiences, studies, research, and opinions regarding a healthy lifestyle. All material included in this publication is believed to be accurate. The publisher assumes no responsibility for any health, welfare, or subsequent damage that might be incurred from use of these materials.

For more information about Healthy Exchanges® products, contact:
Healthy Exchanges, Inc.
P.O. Box 80
DeWitt, Iowa 52742-0080
(563) 659-8234
www.HealthyExchanges.com

PRINTING HISTORY
Perigee trade paperback edition / January 2005

PERIGEE is a registered trademark of Penguin Group (USA) Inc.
The "P" design is a trademark belonging to Penguin Group (USA) Inc.

Library of Congress Cataloging-in-Publication Information

Lund, JoAnna M.
    The Family and friends cookbook : from casserole suppers to champagne celebrations, meal plans, and more than 200 recipes for every occasion / JoAnna M. Lund.
        p.   cm.
    ISBN 0-399-53068-1
    1. Cookery.   I. Title.

TX714.L854 2005
641.5—dc22

2004054494

PRINTED IN THE UNITED STATES OF AMERICA

10   9   8   7   6   5   4   3   2

As all of my books are, this cookbook is dedicated in loving memory to my parents, Jerome and Agnes McAndrews. My mother dearly loved planning menus and sharing unexpected (but pleasant) surprises with her family at mealtime. And, my father enjoyed the surprises every bit as much as my two sisters and I did.

I come from Midwest working-class stock—money was often sparse in our house but the love and caring was abundant! Mom was exceedingly artistic and could "see" in her mind what wonderful wonders she could create for both family and friends from the meager supply of goods stored in her cupboards. Daddy was just as analytical as Mom was artistic. He could "figure" out almost every mathematical problem put his way—which is quite a feat considering he had less than three years of formal education. Farm boys born at the turn of the 20th century often could only get away for schooling during the winter months, and then only if there wasn't other work to be done. My parents were married during the height of the Great Depression but neither of them felt sorry for themselves, even though they didn't have much in material possessions. Instead, they put their earthly talents to good use raising a family of three girls. Luckily, I inherited both Mom's creativity and Daddy's analytical skills and I've put them both to good use when creating this huge collection of festive menus planned for you—be it for family meals or entertaining friends.

In honor of my parents, I want to share a poem my mother wrote many years ago. It speaks of both her creativity and her love for her family. May you enjoy both Mom's words and my menus. My hope is that they will help you share both creativity and love with your family and friends.

Echoes

I am making a colorful braided rug for
  my living room floor
From some old clothing that my three daughters
  and I once proudly wore.
The checkered dress Regina donned for the
  Spelling Bee is still here.
She was awarded third place in Clinton County
  for eighth grade that year.
This is the suit Mary wore to Washington, D.C.
  on her senior class trip
It is no longer in fashion, but almost
  too good to rip.
I am holding the winter coat, once beautiful,
  now faded and torn,
JoAnna bought it with money she earned
  from detasseling corn.
This woolen frock was a favorite of mine,
  the color is royal blue.
My, how pretty I felt when wearing that dress
  back when it was new!
As I stitch together my rug with threads of love,
  moistened with a tear,
Each seam brings back echoes of the past,
  and memories I cherish dear.

by Agnes Carrington McAndrews

Acknowledgments

Putting it all together . . . menu planning that is healthy, tasty, and easy! What makes a meal? How do you put this with that and come up with something that others will rave about? When people comment about the thousands and thousands of "common folk" healthy recipes I've shared in my various cookbooks and newsletters, the question I'm asked more often than not, is "Yes, but how do I put them all together and still get a meal on the table . . . fast?" In this collection of menus I'll show you just how to do that. For helping me so I could help you at mealtime, I want to thank:

Shirley Morrow, Rita Ahlers, Phyllis Bickford, Gina Griep, and Jean Martens—my employees. For the past several months, we've gathered together at lunchtime in my kitchen to try yet another menu I had created. Just like you and your family, each person came to the table with different wants and needs—some needed low-fat; others low-sugar; and others lower-sodium recipes, but all agreed that no matter how healthy a dish was, if it didn't taste good, why bother? Thank goodness all these menus and recipes passed their taste tests with flying colors!

Cliff Lund—my husband, my long-haul trucker, and my business partner. While Cliff is away from home during the week, when he pulls his rig into our driveway on Friday, he knows two things are for sure: He'll have newsletters to print for me; and he'll have a satisfying meal waiting for him when he's done, a supper that is not only good for him but good-tasting, too!

Barbara Alpert—my writing partner. Barbara knows that I love to create recipes and she also knows that I can't spell worth a darn! She takes my words and makes a good book even better. Every writer should be so lucky as to have a Barbara in his or her life!

Coleen O'Shea—my agent. When I mentioned to her that so many people were asking me for help in their menu planning and that I'd really like to write a cookbook on that subject, she did what she so often does—she made my dream a reality!

John Duff—my editor. John agreed that there was indeed room for a menu cookbook on the bookshelf—one featuring comforting meals for both family and friends. As soon as he said yes, my pen and paper went into high gear and I didn't stop until I had all these menus and recipes created!

God—my Creator and Savior. God blesses each and every one of us with talents. He expects us to share with others. Mine happens to be creating recipes that are low enough in fats and sugars to be healthy—but just high enough to be tasty. Praise be to God and pass the food!

Contents

Planning to

Succeed

It's been said that if you fail to plan, you plan to fail—which suggests to me that planning plays a powerful role in helping us reach whatever goals we set for ourselves. Without a plan, we may start to stumble in the direction we wish to go, but it's likely that the path won't be a straight one; we may lose time detouring around unexpected obstacles, and in many cases, we may get lost!

You wouldn't set out to drive cross-country without a road map, and you wouldn't try to set up a new computer without the manual—right? I believe that plotting your journey to a healthy lifestyle and setting up a system that works for you requires a plan, a map, a sheet of instructions, and maybe even a few words of encouragement and inspiration.

So where do you begin?

For me, the best beginnings come with a dream of what I want to accomplish. Healthy Exchanges began with a vision of a life without fear of food, a life in which I had the energy to do all the things I wanted to, a life in which my positive attitude could actually transform my health. I had to figure out how to get what I wanted, and I did make a plan—a plan that evolved into the program that has helped so many people reclaim their health, lose weight, stabilize blood sugar, reduce cholesterol, and discover the energetic person inside!

Start with a List

I remember reading a long time ago in an article about dieting that it was time to forget about "will power" and start depending on "want power" instead. When your choices come from a place of "what you want" rather than a worry about being "in control" or out of it, you're much more likely to keep going, commit to changing your habits, and make healthier choices. So I think it's a good idea to **start with a list of what you want**. Perhaps some of the items on this list may seem trivial, but remember, this list is just for your eyes, no one else's. So if one of the items on it has to do with feeling slim and strong at your daughter's upcoming wedding, that belongs on that list as surely as a desire to lower your blood pressure. When we admit to it, we want lots of things—some big, like losing fifty pounds and getting off medication, and some small ones, like not needing an extension seatbelt anymore when you fly.

A long time ago, I wrote about one of my wishes—to have a pair of pantyhose last more than one wearing. When I was finally able to check that one off, I felt a little explosion of pleasure deep inside. I had been brave enough to say what I wanted—and I had made it happen.

Start writing your list, and add to it over several days. By your willingness to admit that your life could be better, you're already on your way to making that dream a reality.

Examine the Obstacles

Now you want to study the terrain, examining the obstacles that stand between you and your plan to succeed. You've listed "exercise at least three times a week" but you may be worried you don't have the time. In order to find what you can do about that, you'll probably need to plot out how you are spending your time. Can you lift some weights during the commercials of *CSI: Miami?* Is it reasonable to think that you can still enjoy watching *Regis and Kelly* while you are using a mini-trampoline or your manual treadmill? I think it is. (You may need to acquire those weights, mini-trampoline, or treadmill, of course. Garage sales are great for finding them at low prices!)

What other obstacles exist to keep you from where you want to go? When it came to figuring out how to change what I was eating, I had to face my husband and kids, especially their unwillingness to dine on what Cliff so eloquently called "diet slop." I had to find tasty food that was healthy, and all those years ago, I had to make it myself. So I did. More than two dozen cookbooks and my monthly newsletter grew out of that "obstacle," so you'll forgive me if I say with some satisfaction, "Yes, give me a few more of those!"

Line Up Your Team

Don't do it alone if you don't have to. And you don't have to. That's the secret behind much of the success of Weight Watchers, TOPS, First Place, and other weight-loss programs that emphasize group support. Get an exercise buddy to walk with you at 6:30 A.M. if that's going to make the difference, or join CURVES if you've felt intimidated by working out in gyms with macho men. Invite friends to share a few healthy meals each week, because eating alone can be lonely and leave you vulnerable to making unhealthy choices. Plan a shoe-shopping excursion with an office friend during lunch hour instead of eating at your desk—you'll get some fresh air, burn a few calories, and check out the latest trends (remember, you don't *have* to buy!). And if you're someone who has too much free time on your hands and has spent too much of it nibbling in the past, get out of the house and share the wealth of your time. Read with children at a local school, practice English with new immigrants to your town, hold babies in the preemie ward of your hospital. Opportunities abound in every corner of this country, and your contribution to others will bring you more than you give!

Change a Few Habits

Committing to this new healthy living plan may mean giving up a few comfortable habits and replacing them with new behaviors that will help you live and cook healthy. What do I mean? It can be as simple as changing the route you drive to work, so you're not tempted by the fast-food drive-throughs; it can mean picking your lunch the night before so you don't have the excuse of having to hit the nearest coffee shop for a greasy grilled cheese sandwich because you had no time to make it in the morning; and it can mean shifting your scheduled to one that supports your goal of better health.

If you have to trade carpooling days to attend a yoga class, *do it*. If you need to swap lunch hours with a co-worker to fit in a support group meeting, *do it*. And if making your plan work means being a little less available for your kids or your mom, suggest changes that can work for all of you. Make your health a priority, and remember—your life matters to them, so they're likely to jump on the bandwagon when you ask for their help.

I like to say that a habit simply means something we've become accustomed to doing. We can change what we feel is "comfortable" when the prize is worth it—and this time, it truly is.

Plan Some Special Rewards

Part of every successful plan is the bonus program. Businesses do it—why shouldn't you? But instead of frequent flier miles or a set of steak knives to mark a goal, you get to choose your rewards. They don't have to be big ones. They can be as simple as planning a favorite Healthy Exchanges dessert after surviving a sweaty exercise class, as comforting as a long soak in a tub after a Sunday bike ride with your sister, or as satisfying as a phone call to an older friend after watching your favorite movie from college days.

Don't think of rewards as bribes for doing what you said you would do. Instead, consider them as pat on the back we give ourselves for making a plan and sticking to it. Little rewards and special treats make life more enjoyable, and the more you enjoy what you're doing, the more likely you'll keep doing it!

Keep Reviewing Your Goals

It's easy after weeks or months of living your new healthy lifestyle to get distracted or waylaid, to fall off the "Health Wagon" or get discouraged if the numbers on the scale aren't changing fast enough. Don't worry about disappointments or disasters—plan for them! Use those setbacks to re-motivate yourself by reflecting on what you said you wanted. Have those desires changed? Then update your plan, and keep updating it. Maybe you need to add some new goals—fitness goals like finishing a charity walk for breast cancer, cooking goals like training to use a knife like a true chef, learning goals like heading back to school for an advanced degree or to finish your B.A., life goals such as contacting friends with whom you've lost touch, or making peace with a relative you haven't spoken to in years.

Your plan isn't written in stone; it's a living thing that reflects you each step of the way. Add to it, change it, rephrase it, rethink it—and stick with it. Your plan is your road map to your dream!

My Plan for This Book

I've written dozens of cookbooks and created thousands upon thousands of recipes over the years. I think that the question I'm asked most often (after how did I find a gem of a husband like Cliff, my truck drivin' man) is "How do you decide which recipes go together and still get supper on the table . . . fast?"

I know, it can feel overwhelming to be faced with a book full of recipes and a list of ingredients with which to stock your pantry and refrigerator. When you add the sense of urgency that comes with a doctor's prescription to lose weight or face serious medical problems, it's easy to understand why people who start out feeling motivated soon lose steam, miss the exit, take a wrong turn, and end up back where they began—more discouraged than ever!

While most of my cookbooks have included a few suggestions for menus, I've never created a book this comprehensive that's designed just to fill this important need. *Family and Friends Cookbook* features fifty menus for all different occasions. More than forty are what I'm calling weeknight dinners for four or six; there are also splendid Sunday dinners and marvelous menus for entertaining, including buffets, brunches, barbecues, and classic company meals.

You'll find that each menu describes a full meal covering all the nutritional and taste bases; most of the menus include four recipes: a satisfying entrée and a delectable dessert, along with side dishes that complement them. (The menus for entertaining may include as many as eight, with up to two of each, or a half-serving of both in each category.) I've tried to keep the total calorie counts around 500 calories, except for a few special occasions, which go a little higher. (If you're on your own or have a smaller household, don't skip those delightful menus—simply consider them a scenic route to planned leftovers and some lively variety in your life!)

And because everyone may be coming to the table with a different need or concern, these recipes are just right for serving to anyone with diabetes, those interested in counting fat grams or carbs, anyone looking to lose weight and eat a healthier diet, and all those looking to limit cholesterol and consume moderate amounts of sodium.

Now, to make your culinary juggling act as simple and relaxed as possible, the introduction to each menu suggests any preparation you need to do in advance *and* a recommended cooking sequence that will help you bring your dishes to the table all at the same time. I've also revised my popular section on cooking tips to help you cook healthy food every day with ease and pleasure.

From my kitchen to your table—more the two hundred recipes and lots of love!

Jo Anna

Please note—In many of my cookbooks, I've included my Healthy Exchanges eating plan, which explains how to use my version of the "exchange" system for planning what to eat and how much to eat for optimum health and weight loss (or maintenance). Because this is a "special-

interest" cookbook, I've chosen to focus just on menu planning and the recipes for those menus. If this is your first Healthy Exchanges cookbook, please check one of my other cookbooks for an explanation of the exchange system—and an abundance of healthy cooking tips! Good recent choices include The Open Road Cookbook *or* Cooking Healthy with a Man in Mind.

How to Read a Healthy Exchanges Recipe

The Healthy Exchanges Nutritional Analysis

Before using these recipes, you may wish to consult your physician or health-care provider to be sure they are appropriate for you. The information in this book is not intended to take the place of any medical advice. It reflects my experiences, studies, research, and opinions regarding healthy eating.

Each recipe includes nutritional information calculated in three ways:

Healthy Exchanges Weight Loss Choices™ or Exchanges
Calories; Fat, Protein, Carbohydrates, and Fiber in grams;
Sodium and Calcium in milligrams
Diabetic Exchanges

In every Healthy Exchanges recipe, the Diabetic Exchanges have been calculated by a registered dietitian. All the other calculations were done by computer, using the Food Processor II software. When the ingredient listing gives more than one choice, the first ingredient listed is the one used in the recipe analysis. Due to inevitable variations in the ingredients you choose to use, the nutritional values should be considered approximate.

The annotation "(limited)" following Protein counts in some recipes indicates that consumption of whole eggs should be limited to four per week.

Please note the following symbols:

☆ This star means read the recipe's directions carefully for special instructions about **division** of ingredients.

 This symbol indicates **FREEZES WELL.**

The Menus

Meatless
and Fish

Champagne Wishes

Some nights, you dash home from work exhausted and wish that supper could make itself! Believe me, I know that feeling well. On those nights, when it's just Cliff and me, I choose a simple but satisfying menu that still has a little pizzazz. The recipes are quick and tasty, and you wash everything down with my special version of "champagne."

THE PLAN: Start by de-stressing: tearing those spinach leaves into shreds to make **Spinach Sandwiches.** Once they're ready, mix up **Fiesta Champagne** and let it chill before serving. **Grande Tomato Soup** may be the best 5-minute soup you've ever tasted—and while it's simmering, prepare **Sliced Strawberries in Custard Sauce** and place in the fridge while you enjoy a relaxing meal.

Grande Tomato Soup

○ Serves 4 (1 cup)

1 (10¾-ounce) can Healthy Request Tomato Soup
1 (15-ounce) can diced tomatoes, undrained
1 teaspoon chili seasoning
½ cup Land O Lakes Fat Free Half & Half
¼ cup Land O Lakes no-fat sour cream
¼ cup Oscar Mayer or Hormel Real Bacon Bits

In a medium saucepan, combine tomato soup, undrained tomatoes, and chili seasoning. Stir in half & half. Cook over medium heat for 5 minutes or until mixture is heated through, stirring often. When serving, top each bowl with 1 tablespoon sour cream and 1 tablespoon bacon bits.

Each serving equals:

HE: 1 Vegetable • ¼ Fat Free Milk • 1 Slider •
5 Optional Calories

139 Calories • 3 gm Fat • 6 gm Protein •
22 gm Carbohydrate • 624 mg Sodium •
86 mg Calcium • 2 gm Fiber

DIABETIC EXCHANGES: 1 Vegetable •
1 Other Carbohydrate • ½ Meat

Spinach Sandwiches

○ Serves 4

⅓ cup Kraft fat-free mayonnaise
¼ cup Land O Lakes no-fat sour cream
2 tablespoons dried mixed vegetables
2 tablespoons chopped pecans
3 cups finely shredded fresh spinach leaves,
*   stems removed and discarded*
8 slices reduced-calorie white or whole-wheat bread

In a medium bowl, combine mayonnaise, sour cream, dried mixed vegetables, and pecans. Add spinach. Mix well to combine. For each sandwich, spread about ½ cup spinach mixture between 2 slices of bread.

Each serving equals:

HE: 1 Bread • ¾ Vegetable • ½ Fat • ¼ Slider •
8 Optional Calories

---

148 Calories • 4 gm Fat • 7 gm Protein •
21 gm Carbohydrate • 382 mg Sodium •
89 mg Calcium • 2 gm Fiber

DIABETIC EXCHANGES: 1 Starch • 1 Vegetable •
½ Fat

Sliced Strawberries in Custard Sauce

● Serves 4

> 3 cups sliced fresh strawberries
> 1 (4-serving) package JELL-O sugar-free instant vanilla
>   pudding mix
> ⅔ cup Carnation Nonfat Dry Milk Powder
> 1¾ cups water
> ½ teaspoon vanilla extract

Spoon about ¾ cup strawberries into 4 dessert dishes. In a medium bowl, combine dry pudding mix, dry milk powder, and water. Mix well using a wire whisk. Blend in vanilla extract. Spoon a full ½ cup custard sauce over each dish of strawberries. Refrigerate for at least 15 minutes before serving.

Each serving equals:

HE: ¾ Fruit • ½ Fat Free Milk • ¼ Slider •
5 Optional Calories

---

104 Calories • 0 gm Fat • 5 gm Protein •
21 gm Carbohydrate • 363 mg Sodium •
167 mg Calcium • 3 gm Fiber

DIABETIC EXCHANGES: 1 Fruit, ½ Fat Free Milk

Fiesta Champagne

● Serves 4 (1 cup)

1 cup cold Diet Rite White Grape Soda
1 cup cold white grape juice
2 cups cold diet ginger ale

In a large pitcher, combine white grape soda pop and white grape juice. Stir in diet ginger ale. Refrigerate for at least 15 minutes. Good as is or served over ice.

Each serving equals:

HE: ½ Fruit

---

36 Calories • 0 gm Fat • 0 gm Protein •
9 gm Carbohydrate • 31 mg Sodium • 9 mg Calcium •
0 gm Fiber

DIABETIC EXCHANGES: ½ Fruit

Pleased by Cheese

I love the name of this menu, because it's absolutely true—most of us are *so* pleased when a cheesy dish is part of the meal! Why? It's amazingly satisfying, even when your individual serving is no more than 1 ounce. It's rich, even though I use the reduced-fat version— *not* fat-free, though, because it doesn't melt as easily or taste as good, in my opinion. Cheese delivers protein and calcium, too, so it's a terrific part of a healthy diet.

THE PLAN: Any meal is better when chocolate is included, so let's begin with **Fruit Cocktail au Chocolate**, which needs at least an hour to chill. (If you like, make it before you leave for work.) Next, prepare my **Cheesy Pasta Bake in Tomato Sauce**, which requires a few minutes in the skillet and about half an hour in the oven. (Remember that it calls for hot, cooked rotini, so put some water on while you're cooking the sauce.) Let it rest before serving. Fifteen minutes before dinner is served, mix up the dressing for **Lettuce Salad with Spicy Tomato Dressing** and refrigerate. When you're ready to sit down, blend up my fizzy and flavorful **Weeknight Spritzer** and you'll have a great evening.

Cheesy Pasta Bake in Tomato Sauce

🌀 Serves 4

1 (10¾-ounce) can Healthy Request Tomato Soup
1 (8-ounce) can tomatoes, finely chopped and
    undrained
1 (2.5-ounce) jar sliced mushrooms, drained
1½ teaspoons Italian seasoning
¼ cup Kraft Reduced Fat Parmesan Style
    Grated Topping
2 cups hot cooked rotini pasta, rinsed and drained
¾ cup shredded Kraft reduced-fat mozzarella cheese
¾ cup shredded Kraft reduced-fat Cheddar cheese

Preheat oven to 350 degrees. Spray an 8-by-8-inch baking dish with olive oil–flavored cooking spray. In a large skillet, combine tomato soup, undrained tomatoes, mushrooms, and Italian seasoning. Cook over medium heat for 5 minutes or until mixture is heated through, stirring occasionally. Stir in Parmesan cheese topping and rotini pasta. Spread half of mixture in prepared baking dish. In a small bowl, combine mozzarella cheese and Cheddar cheese. Sprinkle 1 cup cheese mixture evenly over pasta mixture. Layer remaining pasta mixture over cheese. Evenly sprinkle remaining ½ cup cheese mixture over top. Cover and bake for 20 minutes. Uncover and continue baking for 10 minutes. Place baking dish on a wire rack and let set for 5 minutes. Divide into 4 servings.

HINT: Usually 1½ cups uncooked rotini pasta cooks to about 2 cups.

Each serving equals:

HE: 2¼ Protein • 1 Bread • ¾ Vegetable • ½ Slider •
5 Optional Calories

281 Calories • 9 gm Fat • 17 gm Protein •
33 gm Carbohydrate • 789 mg Sodium •
328 mg Calcium • 2 gm Fiber

DIABETIC EXCHANGES: 2 Meat • 1 Starch •
½ Vegetable • 1 Other Carbohydrate

Lettuce Salad with Spicy Tomato Dressing

○ Serves 4

½ cup reduced-sodium tomato juice
1 tablespoon finely chopped onion
1 teaspoon lemon juice
½ cup Kraft fat-free mayonnaise
1 teaspoon prepared horseradish sauce
6 cups shredded lettuce

In a small bowl, combine tomato juice, onion, and lemon juice. Add mayonnaise and horseradish sauce. Mix well. Cover and refrigerate for at least 15 minutes. Gently stir again just before serving. For each salad, place 1½ cups lettuce on a plate and drizzle a scant ¼ cup tomato dressing over top. Serve at once.

Each serving equals:

HE: 1¾ Vegetable • ¼ Slider • 2 Optional Calories

44 Calories • 0 gm Fat • 1 gm Protein •
10 gm Carbohydrate • 289 mg Sodium •
46 mg Calcium • 3 gm Fiber

DIABETIC EXCHANGES: 1 Vegetable •
½ Other Carbohydrate

Fruit Cocktail au Chocolate

🗭 Serves 4

> 1 (4-serving) package JELL-O sugar-free chocolate
>   cook-and-serve pudding mix
> ⅔ cup Carnation Nonfat Dry Milk Powder
> 1 cup water
> 1 (15-ounce) can fruit cocktail, packed in fruit juice,
>   drained and ½ cup liquid reserved
> ½ teaspoon coconut extract
> ¼ cup Cool Whip Lite
> 1 tablespoon + 1 teaspoon flaked coconut

In a medium saucepan, combine dry pudding mix, dry milk powder, water, and reserved fruit cocktail juice. Stir in fruit cocktail. Cook over medium heat until mixture thickens and starts to boil, stirring often and being careful not to crush fruit. Remove from heat. Stir in coconut extract. Evenly spoon hot mixture into 4 dessert dishes. Cover and refrigerate for at least 1 hour. When serving, top each with 1 tablespoon Cool Whip Lite and 1 teaspoon coconut.

Each serving equals:

HE: 1 Fruit • ½ Fat Free Milk • ½ Slider •
7 Optional Calories

---

141 Calories • 1 gm Fat • 5 gm Protein •
28 gm Carbohydrate • 171 mg Sodium •
150 mg Calcium • 1 gm Fiber

DIABETIC EXCHANGES: 1 Fruit • ½ Fat Free Milk •
½ Other Carbohydrate

Weeknight Spritzer

○ Serves 4

1 cup cold unsweetened orange juice
1 (8-ounce) can crushed pineapple, packed in fruit juice,
    undrained
2½ cups ice cubes☆
2 cups cold diet ginger ale

In a blender container, combine orange juice, undrained pineapple, and ½ cup ice cubes. Cover and process on BLEND for 20 to 25 seconds or until smooth. Stir in diet ginger ale. For each serving, place ½ cup ice cubes in a tall glass and pour 1 cup spritzer in glass.

Each serving equals:

HE: 1 Fruit

44 Calories • 0 gm Fat • 0 gm Protein •
11 gm Carbohydrate • 27 mg Sodium •
13 mg Calcium • 0 gm Fiber

DIABETIC EXCHANGES: 1 Fruit

Soup and Sandwich

Even if all you have planned is a quick supper before a soccer game or an early movie, you still want to eat well and feel satisfied. You may be astonished to discover you can enjoy a delicious 3-course meal of salad, soup, grilled sandwiches, and a yummy dessert when you've got less than 20 minutes before you have to leave!

THE PLAN: This is one of my fastest menus, ready in almost no time at all. (But check that you've got hard-boiled eggs on hand before you start!) Begin with dessert, because **Fruit Pudding Supreme** will taste more luscious if you give it 15 minutes to get nice and cold. Once it's in the fridge, get started on **Tastes Like Homemade Tomato Soup**. Just pour everything into your saucepan and heat it through (less than 10 minutes). While it's warming, heat up your griddle or skillet and prepare **Egg Salad Toasties**, a family-pleasing and fun way to enjoy this familiar favorite. Now get the **Lettuce Wedges with Homemade Thousand Island Dressing** on the table, and you're on your way!

Lettuce Wedges with Homemade Thousand Island Dressing

⊙ Serves 4

½ cup Kraft fat-free mayonnaise
1 tablespoon reduced-sodium ketchup
1 tablespoon sweet pickle relish
1 teaspoon dried onion flakes
1 hard-boiled egg, chopped
1 small head iceberg lettuce

In a medium bowl, combine mayonnaise, ketchup, pickle relish, and onion flakes. Stir in egg. Cut head of lettuce into 4 wedges. For each serving, place 1 wedge of lettuce on a salad plate and drizzle a scant ¼ cup dressing mixture over each. Serve at once.

Each serving equals:

HE: 1 Vegetable • ¼ Protein • ¼ Slider •
9 Optional Calories

---

62 Calories • 2 gm Fat • 3 gm Protein •
8 gm Carbohydrate • 273 mg Sodium •
23 mg Calcium • 2 gm Fiber

DIABETIC EXCHANGES: 1 Vegetable •
½ Other Carbohydrate

Tastes Like Homemade Tomato Soup

● Serves 4 (1 full cup)

1 (10¾-ounce) can Healthy Request Tomato Soup
2 (15-ounce) cans diced tomatoes, undrained
½ cup Land O Lakes Fat Free Half & Half
1 teaspoon dried parsley flakes
⅛ teaspoon black pepper

In a medium saucepan, combine tomato soup, undrained tomatoes, and half & half. Stir in parsley flakes and black pepper. Cook over medium heat for 6 to 8 minutes or until mixture is heated through, stirring occasionally.

Each serving equals:

HE: 2 Vegetable • ½ Slider • 15 Optional Calories

117 Calories • 1 gm Fat • 3 gm Protein •
24 gm Carbohydrate • 502 mg Sodium •
83 mg Calcium • 4 gm Fiber

DIABETIC EXCHANGES: 2 Vegetable •
½ Other Carbohydrate

Egg Salad Toasties

○ Serves 4

4 hard-boiled eggs, chopped
¼ cup finely chopped celery
¼ cup sweet pickle relish
¼ cup Kraft fat-free mayonnaise
½ teaspoon prepared yellow mustard
1 teaspoon dried parsley flakes
8 slices reduced-calorie whole wheat or white bread
1 egg, slightly beaten, or equivalent in egg substitute
¼ cup fat-free milk
⅛ teaspoon lemon pepper

In a medium bowl, combine chopped eggs, celery, pickle relish, mayonnaise, mustard, and parsley flakes. Spread about ⅓ cup mixture evenly over 4 slices of bread. Top with remaining bread slices. In a shallow dish, combine beaten egg, milk, and lemon pepper. Dip each sandwich on both sides into mixture. Evenly arrange on a hot griddle or skillet sprayed with butter-flavored cooking spray. Cook for 3 to 4 minutes on each side or until golden brown. Serve at once.

Each serving equals:

HE: 1¼ Protein • 1 Bread • ¼ Vegetable • ¼ Slider • 16 Optional Calories

208 Calories • 8 gm Fat • 12 gm Protein • 22 gm Carbohydrate • 528 mg Sodium • 91 mg Calcium • 1 gm Fiber

DIABETIC EXCHANGES: 1 Meat • 1 Starch • ½ Other Carbohydrate

Fruit Pudding Supreme

○ Serves 4

1 (4-serving) package JELL-O sugar-free instant
    banana cream pudding mix
2/3 cup Carnation Nonfat Dry Milk Powder
1 (8-ounce) can crushed pineapple, packed in fruit juice,
    undrained
1 cup water
1/2 cup Cool Whip Free
1/2 teaspoon coconut extract
1 cup (1 medium) diced banana
2 tablespoons chopped pecans
1 tablespoon + 1 teaspoon flaked coconut

In a medium bowl, combine dry pudding mix, dry milk powder, undrained pineapple, and water. Mix well using a wire whisk. Blend in Cool Whip Free and coconut extract. Stir in banana. Evenly spoon pudding mixture into 4 dessert dishes. Sprinkle 1½ teaspoons pecans and 1 teaspoon coconut over top of each. Refrigerate for at least 15 minutes.

HINT: To prevent banana from turning brown, mix with 1 teaspoon lemon juice or sprinkle with Fruit Fresh.

Each serving equals:

HE: 1 Fruit • ½ Fat Free Milk • ½ Fat • ½ Slider •
7 Optional Calories

163 Calories • 3 gm Fat • 5 gm Protein •
29 gm Carbohydrate • 382 mg Sodium •
163 mg Calcium • 2 gm Fiber

DIABETIC EXCHANGES: 1 Fruit • ½ Fat Free Milk •
½ Fat • ½ Other Carbohydrate

Spring Fling

This menu sets your table with a rainbow of colors that remind me of my garden in spring! It's pretty enough to serve to friends, but it makes a lovely family meal, any season at all. I've chosen fruits that are available all year long, and there are no ingredients in the menu that are seasonally "sensitive." Of course, no one will blame you for feeling like kicking up your heels and dancing after dinner!

THE PLAN: Because my **Lemon Chiffon Pie** should chill for at least an hour, you may want to make it ahead—perhaps the night before, as it is ready in just minutes. But if you get home from work with enough time to spare, why not stir it up before taking a refreshing shower and changing into your "comfys"? The rest of the meal needs a bit more than a half hour, so start by mixing up the **Mini Salmon Loaves with Celery Dill Sauce.** While they're baking, prepare the **Creamy Fruit Bowl** and let it chill, then get out the skillet for a quick **Skillet Peas and Pimiento.** Put on some music, set the table, and enjoy the applause!

Creamy Fruit Bowl

○ Serves 4 (½ cup)

> 1 (11-ounce) can mandarin oranges, rinsed and drained
> 1 (8-ounce) can pineapple tidbits, packed in fruit juice,
>   drained and 2 tablespoons liquid reserved
> 1 cup (2 small) cored, unpeeled, and diced Red Delicious apples
> ½ cup miniature marshmallows
> ¼ cup Cool Whip Lite

In a medium bowl, combine mandarin oranges, pineapple, and apples. Stir in reserved pineapple liquid. Add marshmallows. Mix gently to combine. Fold in Cool Whip Lite. Cover and refrigerate for at least 30 minutes. Gently stir again just before serving.

Each serving equals:

HE: 1½ Fruit • ¼ Slider • 18 Optional Calories

121 Calories • 1 gm Fat • 1 gm Protein •
27 gm Carbohydrate • 8 mg Sodium •
10 mg Calcium • 1 gm Fiber

DIABETIC EXCHANGES: 1½ Fruit •
½ Other Carbohydrate

Skillet Peas and Pimiento

○ Serves 4 (½ cup)

½ cup chopped onion
2 cups frozen peas, thawed
1 (2-ounce) jar chopped pimiento, undrained
2 teaspoons I Can't Believe It's Not Butter! Light
    Margarine

In a large skillet sprayed with butter-flavored cooking spray, sauté onion for 5 minutes or until tender. Add peas and undrained pimiento. Mix gently to combine. Stir in margarine. Lower heat, cover, and simmer for 5 minutes, stirring occasionally.

HINT: Thaw peas by placing in a colander and rinsing under hot water for 1 minute.

Each serving equals:

HE: 1 Bread • ¼ Fat • ¼ Vegetable

---

73 Calories • 1 gm Fat • 4 gm Protein •
12 gm Carbohydrate • 106 mg Sodium •
21 mg Calcium • 4 gm Fiber

DIABETIC EXCHANGES: 1 Starch

Mini Salmon Loaves with Celery Dill Sauce

● Serves 4

1 (14.5-ounce) can pink salmon, drained, boned, and flaked
2 slices reduced-calorie white bread, made into crumbs
¼ cup finely chopped onion
¾ cup finely chopped celery
¼ cup Land O Lakes no-fat sour cream
1 (10¾-ounce) can Healthy Request Cream of Celery Soup☆
⅛ teaspoon black pepper
2 tablespoons Kraft fat-free mayonnaise
¼ teaspoon dried dill weed

Preheat oven to 375 degrees. Spray 8 wells of a muffin pan with butter-flavored cooking spray. In a large bowl, combine salmon, bread crumbs, onion, celery, sour cream, 2 tablespoons celery soup, and black pepper. Mix well to combine. Evenly spoon mixture in prepared muffin wells. Bake for 30 to 35 minutes. Place muffin pan on a wire rack and let set for 5 minutes. Meanwhile, in a small saucepan, combine remaining celery soup, mayonnaise, and dill weed. Cook over medium heat for 4 to 5 minutes or until mixture is heated through, stirring often. For each serving, place 2 salmon loaves on a plate and spoon about ¼ cup sauce over top.

Each serving equals:

HE: 3 Protein • ½ Vegetable • ¼ Bread • ¾ Slider • 1 Optional Calorie

216 Calories • 8 gm Fat • 20 gm Protein • 16 gm Carbohydrate • 807 mg Sodium • 269 mg Calcium • 1 gm Fiber

DIABETIC EXCHANGES: 3 Meat • 1 Other Carbohydrate

Lemon Chiffon Pie

● Serves 8

> 1 (4-serving) package JELL-O sugar-free instant vanilla
>   pudding mix
> 1 (4-serving) package JELL-O sugar-free lemon gelatin
> 2/3 cup Carnation Nonfat Dry Milk Powder
> 1 cup water
> 1½ cups Cool Whip Free
> 1 (6-ounce) Keebler graham cracker pie crust
> 2 tablespoons purchased graham cracker crumbs or
>   2 (2½-inch) graham crackers, made into crumbs
> 8 thinly sliced pieces of lemon (optional)

In a large bowl, combine dry pudding mix, dry gelatin, dry milk powder, and water. Mix well using a wire whisk. Gently blend in Cool Whip Free. Evenly spread mixture into pie crust. Sprinkle graham cracker crumbs evenly over top. If desired, garnish with lemon slices. Refrigerate for at least 1 hour. Cut into 8 servings.

HINT: A self-seal sandwich bag works great for crushing graham crackers.

Each serving equals:

HE: 1 Bread • ¼ Fat Free Milk • ¼ Fat • ½ Slider • 5 Optional Calories

166 Calories • 6 gm Fat • 3 gm Protein • 25 gm Carbohydrate • 349 mg Sodium • 75 mg Calcium • 1 gm Fiber

DIABETIC EXCHANGES: 1 Starch • 1 Fat • ½ Other Carbohydrate

It's Time for Tuna

Here's a quick meal that doesn't taste as if you rushed through making it. Tuna is such an economical main dish ingredient, it provides your family with high-quality protein for about a dollar! If you started your New Year by resolving to eat for good health and have at least one meatless meal each week, this is a great menu to have in your repertoire.

THE PLAN: You can make your **Family-Pleasing Tuna Patties** first but wait til just before you're planning to eat to brown and serve them. Make the patties, mix up the sauce, and you're "ready when you're ready!" Next, start your **Herb "Fried" Potatoes,** which add so much to this menu. They take 10 minutes on each side, so allow for that when you put the patties up. **Green Salad with French Celery Dressing** is a delightful starter, and no one will leave the table unhappy after a dish of **Fruit Rhapsody,** a flavorful cousin of old-fashioned ambrosia.

Green Salad with French Celery Dressing

● Serves 4

4 cups torn mixed salad greens or shredded lettuce
½ cup Kraft Fat Free French Dressing
1 tablespoon Kraft fat-free mayonnaise
1 tablespoon Splenda Granular
1 teaspoon celery seed

Evenly arrange 1 cup salad greens on 4 salad plates. In a small bowl, combine French dressing, mayonnaise, Splenda, and celery seed. Drizzle a full 2 tablespoons dressing mixture over each salad. Serve at once.

Each serving equals:

HE: 1 Vegetable • ½ Slider • 9 Optional Calories

60 Calories • 0 gm Fat • 1 gm Protein • 14 gm Carbohydrate • 304 mg Sodium • 39 mg Calcium • 2 gm Fiber

DIABETIC EXCHANGES: 1 Vegetable • ½ Other Carbohydrate

Herb "Fried" Potatoes

● Serves 4 (½ cup)

1 tablespoon + 1 teaspoon I Can't Believe It's Not Butter!
*   Light Margarine*
3 cups diced raw potatoes, rinsed and drained
2 teaspoons dried parsley flakes
2 teaspoons dried onion flakes
½ teaspoon ground oregano
⅛ teaspoon black pepper

In a large skillet sprayed with butter-flavored cooking spray, melt margarine. Evenly arrange potatoes in skillet. Cover and cook on medium for 10 minutes. Lightly spray tops with butter-flavored cooking spray. Carefully turn potatoes. Evenly sprinkle parsley flakes, onion flakes, oregano, and black pepper over top. Cover and continue cooking for 8 to 10 minutes, or until potatoes are browned on the outside and tender inside, stirring occasionally.

Each serving equals:

HE: ¾ Bread • ½ Fat

106 Calories • 2 gm Fat • 2 gm Protein •
20 gm Carbohydrate • 52 mg Sodium •
15 mg Calcium • 2 gm Fiber

DIABETIC EXCHANGES: 1 Starch • ½ Fat

Family-Pleasing Tuna Patties

○ Serves 4

1 teaspoon dried onion flakes
2 tablespoons hot water
1 cup unseasoned dry bread cubes
1 (10¾-ounce) can Healthy Request Cream of Mushroom
     Soup☆
1 egg or equivalent in egg substitute
1 (6-ounce) can white tuna, packed in water,
     drained and flaked
⅓ cup Land O Lakes Fat Free Half & Half
1½ teaspoons dried parsley flakes

In a large bowl, combine onion flakes and water. Add bread cubes, ¼ cup mushroom soup, egg, and tuna. Mix well to combine. Using a ⅓ cup measuring cup as a guide, form into 4 patties. Arrange patties in a large skillet sprayed with butter-flavored cooking spray. Brown patties for 3 to 4 minutes on each side. Meanwhile, in a small saucepan, combine remaining mushroom soup, half & half, and parsley flakes. Cook over medium heat while browning patties, stirring occasionally. When serving, place a tuna patty on a plate and spoon about 3 tablespoons soup mixture over top.

HINT: Pepperidge Farm bread cubes work great.

Each serving equals:

HE: 1¼ Protein • ½ Bread • ½ Slider •
14 Optional Calories

---

144 Calories • 4 gm Fat • 13 gm Protein •
14 gm Carbohydrate • 486 mg Sodium •
118 mg Calcium • 0 gm Fiber

DIABETIC EXCHANGES: 2 Meat • ½ Starch •
½ Other Carbohydrate

Fruit Rhapsody

● Serves 4

2 tablespoons Land O Lakes no-fat sour cream
½ cup Cool Whip Free
½ teaspoon coconut extract
1 cup seedless green grapes
1 (11-ounce) can mandarin oranges, rinsed and drained
1 (8-ounce) can pineapple chunks, packed in fruit juice,
    drained
½ cup miniature marshmallows
1 tablespoon + 1 teaspoon flaked coconut

In a medium bowl, gently combine sour cream, Cool Whip
Free, and coconut extract. Fold in grapes, mandarin oranges,
pineapple chunks, and marshmallows. Evenly spoon mixture into
4 dessert dishes. Top each with 1 teaspoon coconut.

Each serving equals:

HE: 1½ Fruit • ½ Slider • 7 Optional Calories

---

141 Calories • 1 gm Fat • 1 gm Protein •
32 gm Carbohydrate • 23 mg Sodium •
31 mg Calcium • 1 gm Fiber

DIABETIC EXCHANGES: 1½ Fruit •
½ Other Carbohydrate

To Grandmother's House We Go

Now there is just no need to go "over the river and through the woods" to eat well at your grandma's house—you can fix a meal full of happy memories in your very own kitchen! All of these dishes would do a grandma proud, and I can tell you that my own grandkids just loved them, especially dessert.

THE PLAN: **Tropicana Treasure Pie** will taste like the prize it's named for if you give it the time it needs—twice—to get properly cold. Prepare the filling and give it an hour, then allow 15 minutes more before serving. Now, even if your own relatives never made homemade coleslaw, you can! My **Creamy Slaw** just needs a quick stir and a little time to chill before you sit down to dinner. I'd make it before you mix up a delectable version of a family classic, **Grandma's Tuna Noodle Comfort Bake.** While it's baking, heat up your creamy veggie side dish, **Creamed Carrots and Beans.** Your grandma would be proud!

Creamy Slaw

○ Serves 4 (¾ cup)

  ½ cup Kraft fat-free mayonnaise
  1 tablespoon fat-free milk
  2 tablespoons Splenda Granular
  1 teaspoon lemon juice
  ⅛ teaspoon black pepper
  3 cups shredded cabbage
  ½ cup grated carrots

In a large bowl, combine mayonnaise, milk, Splenda, lemon juice, and black pepper. Add cabbage and carrots. Mix well to combine. Cover and refrigerate for at least 30 minutes. Gently stir again just before serving.

HINT: 3½ cups purchased coleslaw mix may be used in place of cabbage and carrots.

Each serving equals:

HE: 1 Vegetable • ¼ Slider • 4 Optional Calories

44 Calories • 0 gm Fat • 1 gm Protein •
10 gm Carbohydrate • 259 mg Sodium •
42 mg Calcium • 2 gm Fiber

DIABETIC EXCHANGES: 1 Vegetable

Creamed Carrots and Beans

❂ Serves 4 (¾ cup)

1 (12-fluid-ounce) can Carnation Evaporated Fat Free Milk
3 tablespoons all-purpose flour
½ teaspoon lemon pepper
1 teaspoon dried parsley flakes
1 (15-ounce) can sliced carrots, rinsed and drained
1 (15-ounce) can cut green beans, rinsed and drained

In a covered jar, combine evaporated milk and flour. Shake well to blend. Pour into a medium saucepan sprayed with butter-flavored cooking spray. Add lemon pepper and parsley flakes. Cook over medium heat until mixture starts to thicken, stirring often. Add carrots and green beans. Mix well to combine. Lower heat and continue cooking for 5 minutes or until heated through, stirring often.

Each serving equals:

HE: 2 Vegetable • ¾ Fat Free Milk • ¼ Bread

132 Calories • 0 gm Fat • 8 gm Protein •
25 gm Carbohydrate • 651 mg Sodium •
277 mg Calcium • 3 gm Fiber

DIABETIC EXCHANGES: 2 Vegetable • 1 Fat Free Milk

Grandma's Tuna Noodle Comfort Bake

○ Serves 4

1 (10¾-ounce) can Healthy Request Cream of Mushroom Soup
1 teaspoon dried onion flakes
1 teaspoon dried parsley flakes
⅛ teaspoon black pepper
2 (6-ounce) cans white tuna, packed in water, drained and flaked
½ cup frozen peas, thawed
1 (2-ounce) jar chopped pimiento, drained
1½ cups hot cooked noodles, rinsed and drained
6 tablespoons shredded Kraft reduced-fat Cheddar cheese

Preheat oven to 350 degrees. Spray an 8-by-8-inch baking dish with butter-flavored cooking spray. In a large bowl, combine mushroom soup, onion flakes, parsley flakes, and black pepper. Stir in tuna, peas, and pimiento. Add noodles. Mix well to combine. Spread mixture evenly into prepared baking dish. Evenly sprinkle Cheddar cheese over top. Bake for 30 to 35 minutes. Place baking dish on a wire rack and let set for 5 minutes. Divide into 4 servings.

HINTS: 1. Thaw peas by placing in a colander and rinsing under hot water for 1 minute.
2. Usually 1¼ cups uncooked noodles cook to about 1½ cups.

Each serving equals:

HE: 2½ Protein • 1 Bread • ½ Slider • 1 Optional Calorie

267 Calories • 7 gm Fat • 27 gm Protein • 24 gm Carbohydrate • 540 mg Sodium • 168 mg Calcium • 1 gm Fiber

DIABETIC EXCHANGES: 3 Meat • 1½ Starch

Tropicana Treasure Pie

○ Serves 8

1 cup seedless green grapes
1 cup (1 medium) diced banana
1 (11-ounce) can mandarin oranges, rinsed and drained
1 (8-ounce) can pineapple tidbits, packed in fruit juice,
    drained and ¼ cup liquid reserved
1 (6-ounce) Keebler graham cracker pie crust
1 (4-serving) package JELL-O sugar-free vanilla
    cook-and-serve pudding mix
1 (4-serving) package JELL-O sugar-free orange gelatin
1 cup Diet Mountain Dew
1 cup Cool Whip Free
½ teaspoon coconut extract
2 tablespoons purchased graham cracker crumbs or
    2 (2½-inch) graham cracker squares, made into crumbs
2 tablespoons flaked coconut
2 tablespoons chopped pecans

In a medium bowl, combine grapes, banana, oranges, and pineapple. Evenly spoon fruit mixture into pie crust. In a medium saucepan, combine dry pudding mix, dry gelatin, reserved pineapple juice, and Diet Mountain Dew. Cook over medium heat until mixture thickens and starts to boil, stirring constantly. Evenly drizzle hot mixture over fruit. Refrigerate for at least 1 hour. In a small bowl, gently combine Cool Whip Free and coconut extract. Spread topping mixture evenly over set filling. In a small bowl, combine graham cracker crumbs, coconut, and pecans. Sprinkle crumb mixture evenly over top. Refrigerate for at least 15 minutes. Cut into 8 servings.

HINT: A self-seal sandwich bag works great for crushing graham
    crackers.

Each serving equals:

HE: 1 Bread • 1 Fruit • ½ Fat • ½ Slider •
1 Optional Calorie

215 Calories • 7 gm Fat • 2 gm Protein •
36 gm Carbohydrate • 217 mg Sodium •
9 mg Calcium • 2 gm Fiber

DIABETIC EXCHANGES: 1 Starch • 1 Fruit • 1 Fat

In the Kitchen with Mom

Some of us are lucky enough to remember childhood afternoons sitting on a stool while Mom did wonderful things with pots and pans (and let us lick the bowl). Not everyone had that experience, I know, but I had Mom in mind when I created this old-fashioned but great-tasting menu of goodies that tastes as if you fussed all day over a hot stove.

THE PLAN: Your starter tonight needs at least 3 hours of refrigerator time to set, so you may want to make it in the morning or even the night before. **Congealed Tomato Salad** sounds a bit strange, but it's my version of a classic aspic and was all the rage in the 1950s. You'll need the oven preheated to 375 degrees for both your entrée and dessert. I'd get your **Tuna Cheese Biscuit Bake** into the oven first, followed by **Mom's Baked Apples.** (You could also make the apples ahead of time and serve them at room temperature or cold.) **Spiced Green Beans** need to simmer on your stovetop and require about 30 minutes all together. This menu is a bit more time-consuming than most of the others in this book, but I believe this meal is well worth it!

Congealed Tomato Salad

◐ Serves 6

½ cup reduced-sodium tomato juice
1 (4-serving) package JELL-O sugar-free lemon gelatin
1 (15-ounce) can diced tomatoes, undrained
½ cup cold water
1 tablespoon dried parsley flakes☆
1 teaspoon dried onion flakes
½ cup finely chopped celery
½ cup Kraft fat-free mayonnaise
1 teaspoon Splenda Granular
1 teaspoon lemon juice
6 lettuce leaves

In a large saucepan, bring tomato juice to a boil. Remove from heat. Add dry gelatin. Mix well to dissolve gelatin. Stir in undrained tomatoes and water. Add 2 teaspoons parsley flakes, onion flakes, and celery. Mix well to combine. Pour mixture into an 8-by-8-inch dish. Refrigerate until firm, about 3 hours. In a small bowl, combine mayonnaise, Splenda, lemon juice, and remaining 1 teaspoon parsley flakes. Evenly spread mixture over set filling. Refrigerate for at least 15 minutes. Cut into 6 pieces. When serving, place 1 lettuce leaf on a salad plate and arrange 1 piece of tomato salad over top.

Each serving equals:

HE: 1 Vegetable • 18 Optional Calories

32 Calories • 0 gm Fat • 1 gm Protein •
7 gm Carbohydrate • 254 mg Sodium •
23 mg Calcium • 2 gm Fiber

DIABETIC EXCHANGES: 1 Vegetable

Spiced Green Beans

● Serves 6 (½ cup)

½ cup chopped onion
¾ cup water
¼ teaspoon ground cinnamon
4 cups frozen cut green beans, thawed
¼ cup reduced-sodium ketchup

In a large skillet sprayed with butter-flavored cooking spray, sauté onion for 5 minutes. Add water and cinnamon. Mix well to combine. Stir in green beans. Lower heat and simmer for 20 minutes or until beans are tender. Stir in ketchup. Continue cooking for 2 to 3 minutes or until mixture is heated through, stirring occasionally.

HINT: Thaw green beans by placing in a colander and rinsing under hot water for 1 minute.

Each serving equals:

HE: 1½ Vegetable • 10 Optional Calories

44 Calories • 0 gm Fat • 1 gm Protein •
10 gm Carbohydrate • 5 mg Sodium •
40 mg Calcium • 3 gm Fiber

DIABETIC EXCHANGES: 1½ Vegetable

Tuna Cheese Biscuit Bake

⚫ Serves 6

1 (7.5-ounce) can Pillsbury refrigerated biscuits
1 (10¾-ounce) can Healthy Request Cream of Mushroom Soup
1 cup fat-free milk
¾ cup shredded Kraft reduced-fat Cheddar cheese
1 tablespoon dried onion flakes
2 teaspoons dried parsley flakes
2 (6-ounce) cans white tuna, packed in water,
      drained and flaked

Preheat oven to 375 degrees. Spray an 8-by-12-inch baking dish with butter-flavored cooking spray. Separate biscuits and cut each into 3 pieces. Evenly arrange biscuit pieces in prepared baking dish. In a medium bowl, combine mushroom soup, milk, Cheddar cheese, onion flakes, and parsley flakes. Add tuna. Mix well to combine. Spoon tuna mixture evenly over biscuit pieces. Bake for 30 to 35 minutes or until biscuits rise to top and are browned. Place baking dish on a wire rack and let set for 5 minutes. Divide into 6 servings.

Each serving equals:

HE: 2 Protein • 1¼ Bread • ½ Slider •
2 Optional Calories

217 Calories • 5 gm Fat • 19 gm Protein •
24 gm Carbohydrate • 718 mg Sodium •
193 mg Calcium • 1 gm Fiber

DIABETIC EXCHANGES: 2½ Meat • 1½ Starch

Mom's Baked Apples

◐ Serves 6

6 small baking apples, cored
½ cup Splenda Granular☆
2 tablespoons I Can't Believe It's Not Butter! Light Margarine
½ teaspoon apple pie spice
2 tablespoons water

Preheat oven to 375 degrees. Spray an 8-by-12-inch baking dish with butter-flavored cooking spray. Evenly arrange apples in prepared baking dish. Spoon 1 teaspoon Splenda and 1 teaspoon margarine in center of each apple. Bake for 30 minutes. In a small bowl, combine remaining 6 tablespoons Splenda, apple pie spice, and water. Evenly spoon mixture over top of apples. Continue baking for 10 minutes or until apples are tender. Place baking dish on a wire rack and let set for at least 5 minutes. Good warm or cold.

Each serving equals:

HE: 1 Fruit • ½ Fat • 8 Optional Calories

78 Calories • 2 gm Fat • 0 gm Protein •
15 gm Carbohydrate • 45 mg Sodium •
8 mg Calcium • 2 gm Fiber

DIABETIC EXCHANGES: 1 Fruit • ½ Fat

Terrific Tuna Casserole

My centerpiece for this menu is that all-American classic, a tuna casserole! I'd bet there are hundreds, maybe thousands of versions of this thrifty, tasty dish that kids love, men adore, and overworked moms choose again and again. I've created plenty of them myself, and as a working mom with three kids, I served many, many, many tuna casseroles over the years. This one pleased my grandkids, who love to help Grandma in the kitchen when they visit.

THE PLAN: Begin with **Creamy Tuna Macaroni Casserole**, stirring all the ingredients together in a nice big bowl before spooning the mixture into your baking dish. While it's baking, put on some dance music and blend up a storm with **Sour Cream Pineapple Cream Cheese Pie**, which you should refrigerate before serving. Then it's time to make **Tantalizing Tomato Salad** and let it chill. **Harvest Green Beans** are the last element in this "terrific" meal, and they can simmer on the stove while you enjoy a quick phone call with a friend.

Tantalizing Tomato Salad

○ Serves 6 (½ cup)

3 cups diced fresh tomatoes
½ cup chopped red onion
¼ cup Kraft Fat Free French Dressing
1 tablespoon Splenda Granular
2 teaspoons chopped freeze-dried chives
1 teaspoon dried basil
1 teaspoon dried dill weed
½ teaspoon celery seed

In a medium bowl, combine tomatoes and onion. In a small bowl, combine French dressing, Splenda, chives, basil, dill weed, and celery seed. Drizzle dressing mixture evenly over tomato mixture. Mix gently just to combine. Cover and refrigerate for at least 15 minutes. Gently stir again just before serving.

Each serving equals:

HE: 1 Vegetable • 16 Optional Calories

40 Calories • 0 gm Fat • 1 gm Protein •
9 gm Carbohydrate • 109 mg Sodium •
17 mg Calcium • 2 gm Fiber

DIABETIC EXCHANGES: 1 Vegetable

Harvest Green Beans

◐ Serves 6 (½ cup)

½ cup finely chopped onion

2 tablespoons apple cider vinegar

2 tablespoons water

2 tablespoons Splenda Granular

⅛ teaspoon black pepper

3 tablespoons Oscar Mayer or Hormel Real Bacon Bits

2 (15-ounce) cans French-style green beans,
    rinsed and drained

In a large skillet sprayed with butter-flavored cooking spray, sauté onion for 5 minutes. Stir in vinegar, water, Splenda, black pepper, and bacon bits. Add green beans. Mix well to combine. Lower heat and simmer for 6 to 8 minutes, stirring occasionally.

Each serving equals:

HE: 1½ Vegetable • 15 Optional Calories

44 Calories • 1 gm Fat • 3 gm Protein •
7 gm Carbohydrate • 381 mg Sodium •
26 mg Calcium • 2 gm Fiber

DIABETIC EXCHANGES: 1½ Vegetable

Creamy Tuna Macaroni Casserole

○ Serves 6

1 (10¾-ounce) can Healthy Request Cream of Mushroom Soup
¼ cup reduced-fat Cheez Whiz
1 teaspoon dried parsley flakes
⅛ teaspoon black pepper
2½ cups cooked elbow macaroni
1 (2-ounce) jar chopped pimiento, drained
2 (6-ounce) cans white tuna, packed in water, drained and flaked
4 (¾-ounce) slices Kraft reduced-fat American cheese
½ cup crushed Lay's "WOW!" potato chips or baked potato chips

Preheat oven to 350 degrees. Spray an 8-by-8-inch baking dish with butter-flavored cooking spray. In a large bowl, combine mushroom soup, Cheez Whiz, parsley flakes, and black pepper. Stir in macaroni and pimiento. Add tuna. Mix well to combine. Spoon mixture into prepared baking dish. Evenly arrange American cheese slices over tuna mixture. Sprinkle crushed potato chips evenly over top. Bake for 30 minutes. Place baking dish on a wire rack and let set 5 minutes. Divide into 6 servings.

HINT: Usually 1⅔ cups uncooked elbow macaroni cooks to about 2½ cups.

Each serving equals:

HE: 2½ Protein • 1 Bread • ¼ Slider •
7 Optional Calories

246 Calories • 6 gm Fat • 22 gm Protein •
26 gm Carbohydrate • 725 mg Sodium •
204 mg Calcium • 1 gm Fiber

DIABETIC EXCHANGES: 2½ Meat • 1 Starch •
½ Other Carbohydrate

Sour Cream Pineapple Cream Cheese Pie

◑ Serves 8

1 (4-serving) package JELL-O sugar-free lemon gelatin
½ cup boiling water
1 (8-ounce) can crushed pineapple, packed in fruit juice, undrained
1 (8-ounce) package Philadelphia fat-free cream cheese
¼ cup Splenda Granular
1 cup Land O Lakes no-fat sour cream
1 (6-ounce) Keebler graham cracker pie crust
2 tablespoons purchased graham cracker crumbs or
2 (2½-inch) graham cracker squares, made into crumbs

In a blender container, combine dry gelatin and boiling water. Cover and process on BLEND for 10 seconds. Add undrained pineapple, cream cheese, and Splenda. Re-cover and process on BLEND for 15 to 20 seconds or until mixture is smooth. Scrape mixture into a large bowl. Fold in sour cream. Spread mixture evenly into pie crust. Evenly sprinkle graham cracker crumbs over top. Refrigerate for at least 30 minutes. Cut into 8 servings.

HINT: A self-seal sandwich bag works great for crushing graham crackers.

Each serving equals:

HE: 1 Bread • ½ Fat • ½ Protein • ¼ Fruit • ½ Slider • 2 Optional Calories

186 Calories • 6 gm Fat • 6 gm Protein • 27 gm Carbohydrate • 305 mg Sodium • 124 mg Calcium • 1 gm Fiber

DIABETIC EXCHANGES: 1 Starch • 1 Fat • ½ Other Carbohydrate

Poultry

It Takes Two

This menu serves four, but each of the dishes features a tantalizing twosome, a powerful partnership that produces some real winners! Think of all those memorable pairs of the past: Gable and Lombard, Hepburn and Tracy, Mickey and Minnie Mouse—you get the idea!

THE PLAN: I'm a Midwestern farm girl at heart, so of course some of my best-loved dishes feature that Iowa staple, corn, plus some prize poultry! Did you know that creamed corn is not off-limits to healthy eaters? Hurray for that, and here I've blended it into a cozy casserole, **Chicken and Corn Bake,** that is just delicious. Once you've slipped it into the oven, it's time to prepare those stars of tables around the world—drumroll, please, for **Peaches and Cream Pudding Treats.** This luscious dessert has a few steps, but the prep work is worth the effort. While dessert chills, you can stir up a charming pair, **Carrot and Green Bean Combo,** and fix a "going for the green" appetizer, **Pea-Cucumber Salad.** It takes two to tango, they say, and two heads are better than one. This menu of perfect pairs proves the point!

Pea-Cucumber Salad

○ Serves 4 (½ cup)

> 1½ cups frozen peas, thawed
> ¾ cup chopped unpeeled cucumber
> ¼ cup chopped celery
> ⅓ cup Kraft fat-free mayonnaise
> 1 tablespoon Splenda Granular
> ½ teaspoon dried dill weed
> ⅛ teaspoon black pepper

In a medium bowl, combine peas, cucumber, and celery. Add mayonnaise, Splenda, dill weed, and black pepper. Mix well to combine. Cover and refrigerate for at least 15 minutes. Gently stir again just before serving.

HINT: Thaw peas by placing in a colander and rinsing under hot water for 1 minute.

Each serving equals:

HE: ¾ Bread • ½ Vegetable • 15 Optional Calories

56 Calories • 0 gm Fat • 3 gm Protein •
11 gm Carbohydrate • 206 mg Sodium •
21 mg Calcium • 3 gm Fiber

DIABETIC EXCHANGES: 1 Starch

Carrot and Green Bean Combo

○ Serves 4 (½ cup)

1½ cups frozen cut green beans, thawed
1½ cups frozen sliced carrots, thawed
1 (2-ounce) jar chopped pimiento, undrained
¼ cup water
1 teaspoon lemon pepper
1 tablespoon + 1 teaspoon I Can't Believe It's Not Butter!
  Light Margarine

In a medium saucepan sprayed with butter-flavored cooking spray, combine green beans, carrots, undrained pimiento, and water. Cover and cook on medium heat for 6 to 8 minutes. Uncover. Stir in lemon pepper and margarine. Continue cooking, uncovered, for 3 to 4 minutes or until vegetables are just tender and most of liquid is absorbed, stirring occasionally.

HINT: Thaw green beans and carrots by placing in a colander and rinsing under hot water for 1 minute.

Each serving equals:

HE: 1½ Vegetable • ½ Fat

58 Calories • 2 gm Fat • 2 gm Protein •
8 gm Carbohydrate • 182 mg Sodium •
37 mg Calcium • 3 gm Fiber

DIABETIC EXCHANGES: 1½ Vegetable • ½ Fat

Chicken and Corn Bake

⚫ Serves 4

½ cup finely chopped onion
1 (15-ounce) can cream-style corn
¼ cup Land O Lakes Fat Free Half & Half
1 egg, beaten, or equivalent in egg substitute
14 small fat-free saltine crackers, made into crumbs
1½ cups diced cooked chicken breast
1 teaspoon dried parsley flakes
⅛ teaspoon black pepper

Preheat oven to 350 degrees. Spray an 8-by-8-inch baking dish with butter-flavored cooking spray. In a large skillet sprayed with butter-flavored cooking spray, sauté onion for 5 minutes. Remove from heat. Stir in corn, half & half, and egg. Add cracker crumbs, chicken, parsley flakes, and black pepper. Mix well to combine. Spread mixture in prepared baking dish. Bake for 25 to 30 minutes. Place baking dish on a wire rack and let set for 5 minutes. Divide into 4 servings.

HINTS: 1. A self-seal sandwich bag works great for crushing crackers.
2. If you don't have leftovers, purchase a chunk of cooked chicken breast from your local deli.

Each serving equals:

HE: 2¼ Protein • 1½ Bread • ¼ Vegetable • 10 Optional Calories

256 Calories • 4 gm Fat • 23 gm Protein • 32 gm Carbohydrate • 502 mg Sodium • 47 mg Calcium • 2 gm Fiber

DIABETIC EXCHANGES: 2 Meat • 1½ Starch

Peaches and Cream Pudding Treats

● Serves 4

1 (4-serving) package JELL-O sugar-free vanilla
    cook-and-serve pudding mix
⅔ cup Carnation Nonfat Dry Milk Powder
1 cup water
1 (15-ounce) can sliced peaches, packed in fruit juice,
    finely chopped, drained, and ½ cup liquid reserved
¼ cup Land O Lakes no-fat sour cream
¼ cup Cool Whip Lite
2 tablespoons chopped pecans

In a medium saucepan, combine dry pudding mix, dry milk powder, water, and reserved peach liquid. Cook over medium heat until mixture thickens and starts to boil, stirring constantly. Remove from heat. Stir in peaches. Place saucepan on a wire rack and let set for 10 minutes. Fold in sour cream. Evenly spoon mixture into 4 dessert or parfait dishes. Refrigerate for at least 15 minutes. When serving, top each with 1 tablespoon Cool Whip Lite and 1½ teaspoons pecans.

Each serving equals:

HE: 1 Fruit • ½ Fat Free Milk • ½ Fat • ½ Slider •
5 Optional Calories

183 Calories • 3 gm Fat • 5 gm Protein •
34 gm Carbohydrate • 207 mg Sodium •
172 mg Calcium • 1 gm Fiber

DIABETIC EXCHANGES: 1 Fruit • ½ Fat Free Milk •
½ Fat • ½ Other Carbohydrate

Fry It in the Oven!

See, I knew that would get your attention! Most of us love the taste of fried foods, but we also understand that most frying requires lots of fat. I have always enjoyed experimenting in the kitchen, and this time out I wanted to find a really good-tasting "fried" chicken dish that never saw the inside of a fryer. Could I do it without all that oil? Could I make it crunchy and tasty and still make it healthy?

Is my name JoAnna? You bet!

THE PLAN: Sometimes a party takes time to "gel," to come together, and this menu is no different. My **Apple Salad Cups** need about 2 hours in the fridge to be at their best, so either start this dinner early or make them ahead. They're quick to prepare! The center-piece of this menu is the **Oven French "Fried" Chicken**, which gets its fabulous flavor from an intriguing combination of ingredients for the coating. Once it's dipped, you'll bake it in the oven while you prepare a pleasant side dish (**Peas and Pimiento**) and a delectable dessert (**Choco-Almond Velvet Puddings**). What a fun and festive meal for young and old!

Apple Salad Cups

○ Serves 4

2 cups Ocean Spray reduced-calorie cranberry juice cocktail☆
1 (4-serving) package JELL-O sugar-free lemon gelatin
½ cup chopped celery
¼ cup chopped walnuts
1 cup (2 small) cored, unpeeled and chopped Red Delicious apples

In a medium saucepan, bring 1 cup cranberry juice cocktail to a boil. Remove from heat. Add dry gelatin. Mix well to dissolve gelatin. Stir in remaining 1 cup cranberry juice cocktail. Add celery, walnuts, and apples. Mix well to combine. Evenly spoon mixture into 4 (12-ounce) custard cups. Refrigerate until firm, about 2 hours.

Each serving equals:

HE: 1 Fruit • ½ Fat • ¼ Protein • ¼ Vegetable •
10 Optional Calories

84 Calories • 4 gm Fat • 1 gm Protein •
11 gm Carbohydrate • 21 mg Sodium •
25 mg Calcium • 1 gm Fiber

DIABETIC EXCHANGES: 1 Fruit • 1 Fat

Peas and Pimiento

○ Serves 4 (½ cup)

2 cups frozen peas, thawed
1 (2-ounce) jar chopped pimiento, undrained
1 teaspoon dried onion flakes
1 teaspoon dried parsley flakes
1 tablespoon + 1 teaspoon I Can't Believe It's Not Butter! Light
*   Margarine*

In a medium saucepan, combine peas and undrained pimiento. Stir in onion flakes, parsley flakes, and margarine. Cook over medium heat for 5 minutes or until mixture is heated through, stirring occasionally.

HINT: Thaw peas by placing in a colander and rinsing under hot water for 1 minute.

Each serving equals:

HE: 1 Bread • ½ Fat

74 Calories • 2 gm Fat • 4 gm Protein •
10 gm Carbohydrate • 128 mg Sodium •
19 mg Calcium • 3 gm Fiber

DIABETIC EXCHANGES: 1 Starch • 1 Fat

Oven French "Fried" Chicken

Serves 4

½ cup Kraft Fat Free French Dressing
1 teaspoon dried parsley flakes
⅛ teaspoon black pepper
1 cup crushed Lay's "WOW!" or baked potato chips
16 ounces skinned and boned uncooked chicken breast,
   cut into 4 pieces

Preheat oven to 350 degrees. Spray an 8-by-8-inch baking dish with butter-flavored cooking spray. In a shallow saucer, combine French dressing, parsley flakes, and black pepper. Place crushed potato chips in another saucer. Dip chicken pieces first into dressing mixture, then into potato chips. Evenly arrange chicken pieces in prepared baking dish. Drizzle any remaining dressing mixture and potato chips evenly over top of chicken pieces. Bake for 40 to 45 minutes or until chicken is thoroughly cooked. Place baking dish on a wire rack and let set for 5 minutes. Divide into 4 servings.

Each serving equals:

HE: 3 Protein • ¾ Bread • ½ Slider •
5 Optional Calories

228 Calories • 4 gm Fat • 27 gm Protein •
21 gm Carbohydrate • 470 mg Sodium •
14 mg Calcium • 1 gm Fiber

DIABETIC EXCHANGES: 3 Meat •
1½ Other Carbohydrate

Choco-Almond Velvet Puddings

○ Serves 4

> 1 (4-serving) package JELL-O sugar-free instant chocolate
>   pudding mix
> ⅔ cup Carnation Nonfat Dry Milk Powder
> 1½ cups water
> ½ cup Cool Whip Free
> ½ teaspoon almond extract
> ¼ cup slivered almonds, toasted

In a medium bowl, combine dry pudding mix, dry milk powder, and water. Mix well using a wire whisk. Blend in Cool Whip Free and almond extract. Evenly spoon mixture into 4 dessert dishes. Sprinkle 1 tablespoon almonds over top. Refrigerate for at least 15 minutes.

HINT: To toast almonds, spread in a glass pie plate and microwave on HIGH (100 percent power) for 6 to 7 minutes or until golden. Stir after the first three minutes, then each minute after, until done.

Each serving equals:

HE: ½ Fat Free Milk • ½ Fat • ¼ Protein •
½ Slider • 5 Optional Calories

132 Calories • 4 gm Fat • 6 gm Protein •
18 gm Carbohydrate • 368 mg Sodium •
168 mg Calcium • 1 gm Fiber

DIABETIC EXCHANGES: 1 Fat Free Milk • 1 Fat •
½ Other Carbohydrate

Spring Chicken Sensation

I was thinking seasonally when I titled this menu, but perhaps it also will make anyone feel young and passionate again! So even if you're "no spring chicken" anymore, this magnificent meal will put a bit of spring into your step. Because it features both strawberries and asparagus, it's perfect for a May or June meal (Graduation? Anniversary? You decide!).

THE PLAN: Dessert is a great place to begin for this meal, and the gorgeous green of **Key Lime Chiffon Pie** is enough to get you singing. While it chills, you can start your entrée, lovely **Chicken à la Asparagus,** which requires time in the skillet and a bit of preparation for the sauce. Your **Noodle Side Dish** is ready in minutes, as is an irresistible **Strawberry Lettuce Salad.** You'll have a beautiful meal to share with those you love best!

Strawberry Lettuce Salad

◐ Serves 4

3 tablespoons strawberry spreadable fruit
2 tablespoons white distilled vinegar
2 tablespoons Diet Mountain Dew
2 tablespoons Splenda Granular
4 cups torn mixed salad greens
1 cup chopped fresh strawberries
¼ cup chopped walnuts

In a small bowl, combine spreadable fruit, vinegar, Diet Mountain Dew, and Splenda. For each salad, place 1 cup salad greens on a plate, arrange ¼ cup strawberries over lettuce, drizzle a scant 2 tablespoons dressing mixture over top, and garnish with 1 tablespoon walnuts.

Each serving equals:

HE: 1 Fruit • 1 Vegetable • ½ Fat • ¼ Protein •
3 Optional Calories

105 Calories • 5 gm Fat • 2 gm Protein •
13 gm Carbohydrate • 15 mg Sodium •
43 mg Calcium • 3 gm Fiber

DIABETIC EXCHANGES: 1 Fruit • 1 Vegetable • 1 Fat

Noodle Side Dish

● Serves 4 (¾ cup)

> *2 cups hot cooked noodles, rinsed and drained*
> *¼ cup Kraft Reduced Fat Parmesan Style Grated Topping*
> *¼ cup Land O Lakes Fat Free Half & Half*
> *1 tablespoon + 1 teaspoon I Can't Believe It's Not Butter! Light*
>   *Margarine*
> *⅛ teaspoon black pepper*

In a medium saucepan, combine noodles, Parmesan cheese, and half & half. Stir in margarine and black pepper. Cook over medium heat for 4 to 5 minutes or until mixture is heated through, stirring often.

HINT: Usually 1¾ cups uncooked noodles cooks to about 2 cups.

Each serving equals:

HE: 1 Bread • ½ Fat • ¼ Protein •
10 Optional Calories

152 Calories • 4 gm Fat • 5 gm Protein •
24 gm Carbohydrate • 172 mg Sodium •
80 mg Calcium • 1 gm Fiber

DIABETIC EXCHANGES: 1½ Starch • ½ Fat

Chicken à la Asparagus

○ Serves 4

16 ounces skinned and boned uncooked chicken breast,
  cut into 4 pieces
3 tablespoons all-purpose flour
1 tablespoon + 1 teaspoon I Can't Believe It's Not Butter!
  Light Margarine
½ cup Kraft fat-free mayonnaise
1½ teaspoons prepared yellow mustard
2 tablespoons Land O Lakes Fat Free Half & Half
1 teaspoon dried parsley flakes
1½ teaspoons lemon juice
⅛ teaspoon black pepper
12 asparagus spears, cooked, rinsed, and cooled

Flatten chicken pieces, using a meat cleaver. In a shallow bowl, coat chicken pieces in flour. In a large skillet sprayed with butter-flavored cooking spray, melt margarine. Add chicken pieces. Sprinkle any remaining flour evenly over top. Brown chicken pieces for 4 to 5 minutes on each side or until chicken is browned and cooked through. Meanwhile, in a small saucepan, combine mayonnaise, mustard, half & half, parsley flakes, lemon juice, and black pepper. Cook over medium heat for 4 to 5 minutes or until chicken is cooked and mixture is heated through. For each serving, place a chicken piece on a plate, arrange 3 cooled asparagus spears over chicken, and drizzle about 2 tablespoons mayonnaise mixture over top.

Each serving equals:

HE: 3 Protein • ½ Fat • ¼ Bread • ¼ Vegetable •
¼ Slider • 5 Optional Calories

189 Calories • 5 gm Fat • 25 gm Protein •
11 gm Carbohydrate • 373 mg Sodium •
38 mg Calcium • 1 gm Fiber

DIABETIC EXCHANGES: 3 Meat • ½ Fat

Key Lime Chiffon Pie

○ Serves 8

1 (4-serving) package JELL-O sugar-free lime gelatin

¾ cup Diet Mountain Dew

1½ cups Dannon plain fat-free yogurt

1 (4-serving) package JELL-O sugar-free instant vanilla
    pudding mix

⅔ cup Carnation Nonfat Dry Milk Powder

1 (6-ounce) Keebler graham cracker pie crust

1 cup Cool Whip Lite

2 tablespoons purchased graham cracker crumbs or
    2 (2½-inch) graham cracker squares, made into crumbs

In a large bowl, combine dry gelatin and Diet Mountain Dew. Stir in yogurt. Add dry pudding mix and dry milk powder. Mix well using a wire whisk. Spread mixture evenly into pie crust. Refrigerate for 5 minutes. Carefully spread Cool Whip Lite over set filling. Evenly sprinkle graham cracker crumbs over top. Refrigerate for at least 30 minutes. Cut into 8 servings.

HINT: A self-seal sandwich bag works great for crushing graham crackers.

Each serving equals:

HE: 1 Bread • ½ Fat Free Milk • ¼ Fat • ½ Slider •
2 Optional Calories

182 Calories • 6 gm Fat • 6 gm Protein •
26 gm Carbohydrate • 379 mg Sodium •
167 mg Calcium • 1 gm Fiber

DIABETIC EXCHANGES: 1 Starch • 1 Fat •
½ Fat Free Milk • ½ Other Carbohydrate

Fiesta Fun

I've always believed that your eyes begin "eating" long before a single bite enters your mouth. I'm convinced that true satisfaction comes as much from how a meal looks as how it tastes. For this reason, I love cooking Mexican-style. Dishes that originate in that culture are almost always colorful and full of fresh ingredients that intensify flavor. When Mexicans party, they call it *fiesta*, and so I invite you to celebrate anything and everything with this sweetly spicy menu.

THE PLAN: Attention, please! In order for this celebration to be just perfect, you'll need to make **South of the Border Marinated Veggie Salad** at least 8 hours in advance. (I suggest the night before—it'll take just a minute or two to combine the ingredients.) On the day of your fiesta meal, you'll be delighted at how quickly and easily **Hacienda Chicken Bake** gets ready for the oven. Mix up **Fiesta Chocolate Almond Pudding** next and refrigerate before serving. Finally, get out the skillet and finish your festive meal with **Grande Garden Pilaf**, a lively rice dish. Cheers for the chef—olé!

South of the Border Marinated Veggie Salad

◐ Serves 4 (1 cup)

½ cup Kraft Fat Free Catalina Dressing
¼ cup Splenda Granular
¼ cup white distilled vinegar
1 tablespoon chopped fresh parsley or 1 teaspoon
    dried parsley flakes
1 cup sliced carrots
1 cup chopped fresh cauliflower
1 cup chopped fresh broccoli
½ cup chopped onion

In a large bowl, combine Catalina dressing, Splenda, vinegar, and parsley. Add carrots, cauliflower, broccoli, and onion. Mix well to combine. Cover and refrigerate for at least 8 hours or overnight. Will keep for up to a week in refrigerator.

Each serving equals:

HE: 1¾ Vegetable • ½ Slider • 1 Optional Calorie

68 Calories • 0 gm Fat • 1 gm Protein •
16 gm Carbohydrate • 284 mg Sodium •
27 mg Calcium • 3 gm Fiber

DIABETIC EXCHANGES: 1 Vegetable •
½ Other Carbohydrate

Grande Garden Pilaf

○ Serves 4 (1 cup)

1½ cups shredded unpeeled zucchini
1 cup shredded carrots
½ cup chopped onion
1 (14-ounce) can Swanson Lower Sodium Fat Free
    Chicken Broth
1 teaspoon chili seasoning
⅛ teaspoon black pepper
1⅓ cups uncooked instant rice

In a large skillet sprayed with butter-flavored cooking spray, sauté zucchini, carrots, and onion for 6 to 8 minutes. Add chicken broth, chili seasoning, and black pepper. Mix well to combine. Stir in uncooked instant rice. Bring mixture to a boil. Lower heat, cover, and simmer for 12 to 15 minutes or until rice is tender and most of liquid is absorbed, stirring occasionally.

Each serving equals:

HE: 1½ Vegetable • 1 Bread • 8 Optional Calories

140 Calories • 0 gm Fat • 5 gm Protein •
30 gm Carbohydrate • 209 mg Sodium •
29 mg Calcium • 2 gm Fiber

DIABETIC EXCHANGES: 1½ Vegetable • 1½ Starch

Hacienda Chicken Bake

○ Serves 4

3 tablespoons all-purpose flour

1 teaspoon chili seasoning

1 teaspoon dried parsley flakes

16 ounces skinned and boned uncooked chicken breast,
*   cut into 4 pieces*

1 (10¾-ounce) can Healthy Request Cream of Chicken Soup

½ cup chunky salsa (mild, medium, or hot)

¼ cup sliced ripe olives

¼ cup Land O Lakes no-fat sour cream

Preheat oven to 350 degrees. Spray an 8-by-8-inch baking dish with butter-flavored cooking spray. In a shallow saucer, combine flour, chili seasoning, and parsley flakes. Coat chicken pieces on both sides with flour mixture. Evenly arrange chicken pieces in prepared baking dish. In a medium bowl, combine chicken soup, salsa, olives, and any remaining flour mixture. Spoon soup mixture evenly over chicken pieces. Bake for 45 to 50 minutes or until chicken is tender. When serving, evenly spoon sauce over chicken pieces and top each with 1 tablespoon sour cream.

Each serving equals:

HE: 3 Protein • ¼ Bread • ¼ Fat • ¼ Vegetable • ¾ Slider

---

221 Calories • 5 gm Fat • 26 gm Protein • 18 gm Carbohydrate • 558 mg Sodium • 41 mg Calcium • 1 gm Fiber

---

DIABETIC EXCHANGES: 3 Meat • 1 Other Carbohydrate

Fiesta Chocolate Almond Pudding

○ Serves 4

1 (4-serving) package JELL-O sugar-free instant chocolate
    pudding mix
⅔ cup Carnation Nonfat Dry Milk Powder
1½ cups water
½ cup Cool Whip Free
1 teaspoon almond extract
½ teaspoon ground cinnamon
2 tablespoons slivered almonds

In a medium bowl, combine dry pudding mix, dry milk powder, and water. Mix well using a wire whisk. Gently blend in Cool Whip Free, almond extract, and cinnamon. Evenly spoon mixture into 4 dessert dishes. Top each with 1½ teaspoons almonds. Refrigerate for at least 15 minutes.

Each serving equals:

HE: ½ Fat Free Milk • ¼ Fat • ½ Slider •
9 Optional Calories

110 Calories • 2 gm Fat • 6 gm Protein •
17 gm Carbohydrate • 367 mg Sodium •
161 mg Calcium • 1 gm Fiber

DIABETIC EXCHANGES: ½ Fat Free Milk • ½ Fat •
½ Other Carbohydrate

Italian Holiday

Got your tickets on Alitalia? Are your suitcases packed and ready for a journey to the land that gave us *la dolce vita,* "the sweet life"? Even if you haven't got, current plans to say "Ciao!" to your hometown and jet off for a Roman holiday, you can enjoy a culinary ramble through the flavors of that passionate peninsula!

THE PLAN: You've got two hot dishes to prepare this evening, but you can work on one while the other bakes. Start with **Green Bean and Potato Scallop,** which is ready for the oven in moments. Then you can focus on your **Parmesan Tomato Chicken.** You'll bake the chicken pieces while you make the scrumptious sauce. Spoon it over the chicken, add the cheese, and let it finish baking while you create a gorgeous **Pear Pistachio Pudding** for dessert. **Italian Side Salad** is a colorful starter that will surely put you and your loved ones in the mood!

Italian Side Salad

○ Serves 4 (1¼ cups)

6 cups torn mixed salad greens
1 cup cherry tomatoes
¼ cup sliced ripe olives
½ cup Kraft Fat Free Italian Dressing
1 tablespoon Splenda Granular

In a large bowl, combine salad greens, tomatoes, and olives. In a small bowl, combine Italian dressing and Splenda. Drizzle dressing mixture evenly over salad mixture. Toss gently to coat. Serve at once.

Each serving equals:

HE: 2 Vegetable • ¼ Fat • 17 Optional Calories

49 Calories • 1 gm Fat • 2 gm Protein •
8 gm Carbohydrate • 485 mg Sodium •
67 mg Calcium • 2 gm Fiber

DIABETIC EXCHANGES: 2 Vegetable

Green Bean and Potato Scallop

🖤 Serves 4

3 cups shredded loose-packed frozen potatoes
2 cups frozen cut green beans, thawed
1 (10¾-ounce) can Healthy Request Cream of Mushroom Soup
2 teaspoons dried onion flakes
1 teaspoon dried parsley flakes
1 teaspoon lemon pepper
5 Reduced Fat Ritz Crackers, made into crumbs

Preheat oven to 425 degrees. Spray an 8-by-8-inch baking dish with butter-flavored cooking spray. In a large bowl, combine potatoes and green beans. Add mushroom soup, onion flakes, parsley flakes, and lemon pepper. Mix well to combine. Spread mixture evenly into prepared baking dish. Evenly sprinkle cracker crumbs over top. Lightly spray top with butter-flavored cooking spray. Bake for 30 minutes. Place baking dish on a wire rack and let set for 5 minutes. Divide into 4 servings.

HINTS: 1. Thaw green beans by placing in a colander and rinsing under hot water for 1 minute.
2. A self-seal sandwich bag works great for crushing crackers.

Each serving equals:

HE: 1 Vegetable • ¾ Bread • ½ Slider •
1 Optional Calorie

150 Calories • 2 gm Fat • 5 gm Protein •
28 gm Carbohydrate • 406 mg Sodium •
102 mg Calcium • 3 gm Fiber

DIABETIC EXCHANGES: 1 Vegetable • 1 Starch •
½ Other Carbohydrate

Parmesan Tomato Chicken

● Serves 4

16 ounces skinned and boned uncooked chicken breast,
  cut into 4 pieces
1 (15-ounce) can diced tomatoes, undrained
2 tablespoons cornstarch
1 tablespoon Splenda Granular
1½ teaspoons Italian seasoning
¼ cup Kraft Reduced Fat Parmesan Style Grated Topping

Preheat oven to 425 degrees. Spray an 8-by-8-inch baking dish with butter-flavored cooking spray. Evenly arrange chicken pieces in prepared baking dish. Cover and bake for 15 minutes. Drain chicken, if necessary. Meanwhile, in a medium saucepan, combine undrained tomatoes, cornstarch, Splenda, and Italian seasoning. Cook over medium heat until mixture thickens, stirring constantly. Spoon hot sauce over chicken pieces. Evenly sprinkle Parmesan cheese over sauce. Continue baking, uncovered, for 15 minutes. When serving, evenly spoon sauce over chicken pieces.

Each serving equals:

HE: 3¼ Protein • 1 Vegetable • 16 Optional Calories

189 Calories • 5 gm Fat • 24 gm Protein •
12 gm Carbohydrate • 276 mg Sodium •
73 mg Calcium • 2 gm Fiber

DIABETIC EXCHANGES: 3 Meat • 1 Vegetable

Pear Pistachio Pudding

🌀 Serves 4

1 (4-serving) package JELL-O sugar-free instant pistachio
    pudding mix
⅔ cup Carnation Nonfat Dry Milk Powder
1 (15-ounce) can pear halves, packed in fruit juice,
    chopped, drained, and ½ cup liquid reserved
1 cup water
½ cup Cool Whip Lite
4 (2½-inch) chocolate graham crackers, made into fine crumbs

In a medium bowl, combine dry pudding mix, dry milk powder, reserved pear liquid, and water. Mix well using a wire whisk. Blend in ¼ cup Cool Whip Lite. Gently stir in chopped pears. Evenly spoon mixture into 4 dessert dishes. Sprinkle about 1 tablespoon graham cracker crumbs over each. Top each with 1 tablespoon Cool Whip Lite. Refrigerate for at least 15 minutes.

HINT: A self-seal sandwich bag works great for crushing graham
    crackers.

Each serving equals:

HE: 1 Fruit • ½ Fat Free Milk • ¼ Bread •
½ Slider • 5 Optional Calories

154 Calories • 2 gm Fat • 4 gm Protein •
30 gm Carbohydrate • 382 mg Sodium •
150 mg Calcium • 1 gm Fiber

DIABETIC EXCHANGES: 1 Fruit • ½ Fat Free Milk •
½ Other Carbohydrate

Doing the Continental

At one time, the height of sophistication and glamour meant doing things the "Continental" way, as they were done over in the Europe in the early years of the twentieth century. I'm happy to tell you that you don't have to break out your tuxedo and ballgown to sit down to this dinner, although if you feel like dressing up a bit, you'll get no argument from me.

THE PLAN: Just coat your chicken pieces and start browning them to make **Chicken Garden Skillet** while you prepare its tasty sauce. Pour it over, simmer for about 20 minutes, and you've got an entrée to be justly proud of. Dessert is easy, a **Coconut Lemon Cream,** that should be chilled before serving. A few minutes in the skillet, and **Olive and Noodle Side Dish** is ready to go. Call the family to dinner, mix up your **Continental Tossed Salad,** and you're on your way!

Continental Tossed Salad

● Serves 4 (1¼ cups)

4 cups finely shredded lettuce
1 cup diced fresh tomato
¼ cup chopped green onion
¾ cup sliced fresh mushrooms
½ cup Kraft Fat Free French Dressing
2 tablespoons Kraft fat-free mayonnaise
1 (2-ounce) jar chopped pimiento, drained
1½ teaspoons dried parsley flakes

In a large bowl, combine lettuce, tomato, green onion, and mushrooms. In a small bowl, combine French dressing, mayonnaise, pimiento, and parsley flakes. Drizzle dressing mixture evenly over lettuce mixture. Toss gently to coat. Serve at once.

Each serving equals:

HE: 2 Vegetable • ½ Slider • 15 Optional Calories

84 Calories • 0 gm Fat • 2 gm Protein •
19 gm Carbohydrate • 408 mg Sodium •
32 mg Calcium • 4 gm Fiber

DIABETIC EXCHANGES: 2 Vegetable •
½ Other Carbohydrate

Olive and Noodle Side Dish

○ Serves 4 (½ cup)

> 2 cups hot cooked noodles, rinsed and drained
> ¼ cup Land O Lakes Fat Free Half & Half
> 1 tablespoon + 1 teaspoon I Can't Believe It's Not Butter!
>   Light Margarine
> ¼ cup Kraft Reduced Fat Parmesan Style Grated Topping
> ¼ cup chopped ripe olives

In a medium saucepan, combine noodles, half & half, and margarine. Stir in Parmesan cheese and olives. Cook over medium-low heat for 5 to 6 minutes or until mixture is heated through, stirring often.

HINT: Usually 1¾ cups uncooked noodles cooks to about 2 cups.

Each serving equals:

HE: 1 Bread • ¾ Fat • ¼ Protein •
10 Optional Calories

---

161 Calories • 5 gm Fat • 5 gm Protein •
24 gm Carbohydrate • 214 mg Sodium •
86 mg Calcium • 1 gm Fiber

DIABETIC EXCHANGES: 1½ Starch • 1 Fat

Chicken Garden Skillet

○ Serves 4

3 tablespoons all-purpose flour
1 teaspoon dried parsley flakes
⅛ teaspoon black pepper
16 ounces skinned and boned uncooked chicken breast,
*   cut into 4 pieces*
1 (10¾-ounce) can Healthy Request Cream of Chicken Soup
1 (15-ounce) can diced tomatoes, undrained
¾ cup chopped onion
½ cup chopped green bell pepper

In a shallow saucer, combine flour, parsley flakes, and black pepper. Evenly coat chicken pieces with flour mixture. Arrange coated chicken pieces in a large skillet sprayed with butter-flavored cooking spray. Brown chicken for 3 to 4 minutes on each side. In a medium bowl, combine chicken soup, undrained tomatoes, onion, green pepper, and any remaining flour mixture. Pour mixture evenly over chicken. Lower heat, cover, and simmer for 20 minutes or until vegetables are tender, stirring occasionally. When serving, evenly spoon sauce over chicken pieces.

Each serving equals:

HE: 3 Protein • 1½ Vegetable • ¼ Bread • ½ Slider •
5 Optional Calories

220 Calories • 4 gm Fat • 26 gm Protein •
20 gm Carbohydrate • 456 mg Sodium •
37 mg Calcium • 3 gm Fiber

DIABETIC EXCHANGES: 3 Meat • 1½ Vegetable •
1 Other Carbohydrate

Coconut Lemon Cream

○ Serves 4

1 (4-serving) package JELL-O sugar-free instant vanilla
    pudding mix
1 (4-serving) package JELL-O sugar-free lemon gelatin
⅔ cup Carnation Nonfat Dry Milk Powder
1½ cups Diet Mountain Dew
½ cup Cool Whip Free
½ teaspoon coconut extract
2 tablespoons purchased graham cracker crumbs or
    2 (2½-inch) graham cracker squares, made into crumbs
2 tablespoons flaked coconut

In a medium bowl, combine dry pudding mix, dry gelatin, dry milk powder, and Diet Mountain Dew. Mix well using a wire whisk. Gently blend in Cool Whip Free and coconut extract. Evenly spoon mixture into 4 dessert or parfait dishes. In a small bowl, combine graham cracker crumbs and coconut. Sprinkle about 1 tablespoon crumb mixture evenly over top of each. Refrigerate for at least 15 minutes.

HINT: A self-seal sandwich bag works great for crushing graham crackers.

Each serving equals:

HE: ½ Fat Free Milk • ¾ Slider • 11 Optional Calories

105 Calories • 1 gm Fat • 6 gm Protein •
18 gm Carbohydrate • 454 mg Sodium •
151 mg Calcium • 0 gm Fiber

DIABETIC EXCHANGES: 1 Other Carbohydrate •
½ Fat Free Milk

Cozy Chicken Dinner

I considered including this meal in the "Entertaining" chapter because it's fabulous enough to serve to guests or for a very special occasion. But it's also, like its namesake, a homey sort of dinner that is perfect anytime at all. So why not treat yourself like company and make it a regular on your table? It takes a little extra time, but the results are spectacular, especially dessert!

THE PLAN: Now don't worry just because you've never made something like my **Ice Cream Cake Roll** before—it's not that difficult! It does take some effort, and it needs to chill for at least 2 hours, so make sure you leave enough time or do it ahead. Get all your ingredients ready before you begin, and double check that you've got everything. You'll need a clean dishtowel, aluminum foil, and waxed paper to help you make the cake, so have those items ready as well. Have fun! While dessert is in the freezer, get the **Bountiful Chicken and Dressing** ready. (Allow about an hour from start to finish for this entrée—it has several steps.) While it bakes, you can finish your preparations by stirring up **Skillet Peas with Mushrooms** and **Dilled Stewed Tomatoes.** This is a real "honey-do" menu, so think about using it when you've got some special project for your "honey!"

Skillet Peas with Mushrooms

○ Serves 4 (½ cup)

½ cup finely chopped onion

2 cups frozen peas, thawed

1 (2.5-ounce) jar sliced mushrooms, drained

2 teaspoons Splenda Granular

⅛ teaspoon black pepper

1 tablespoon + 1 teaspoon I Can't Believe It's Not Butter!
   Light Margarine

In a medium skillet sprayed with butter-flavored cooking spray, sauté onion for 5 minutes. Stir in peas and mushrooms. Add Splenda, black pepper, and margarine. Mix well to combine. Lower heat and simmer for 5 to 6 minutes, stirring occasionally.

HINT: Thaw peas by placing in a colander and rinsing under hot water for 1 minute.

Each serving equals:

HE: 1 Bread • ½ Fat • ½ Vegetable •
1 Optional Calorie

---

86 Calories • 2 gm Fat • 4 gm Protein •
13 gm Carbohydrate • 181 mg Sodium •
23 mg Calcium • 4 gm Fiber

DIABETIC EXCHANGES: 1 Starch • ½ Fat • ½ Vegetable

Dilled Stewed Tomatoes

○ Serves 4 (½ cup)

¼ cup finely chopped onion
1 (15-ounce) can diced tomatoes, undrained
1 tablespoon Splenda Granular
½ teaspoon dried dill weed
2 slices reduced-calorie white bread, torn into pieces

In a medium saucepan sprayed with butter-flavored cooking spray, sauté onion for 5 minutes. Stir in undrained tomatoes, Splenda, and dill weed. Add bread pieces. Mix well to combine. Lower heat and simmer for 5 minutes or until mixture is heated through, stirring occasionally.

Each serving equals:

HE: 1 Vegetable • ¼ Bread • 2 Optional Calories

---

52 Calories • 0 gm Fat • 2 gm Protein •
11 gm Carbohydrate • 181 mg Sodium •
31 mg Calcium • 2 gm Fiber

DIABETIC EXCHANGES: 1 Vegetable

Bountiful Chicken and Dressing

◐ Serves 4

16 ounces skinned and boned uncooked chicken breast,
*   cut into 4 pieces*
8 slices reduced-calorie white bread, toasted and cubed
1 cup finely chopped celery
½ cup finely chopped onion
1 (10¾-ounce) can Healthy Request Cream of Chicken Soup☆
½ cup water
1 teaspoon ground sage
⅛ teaspoon black pepper

Preheat oven to 350 degrees. Spray an 8-by-8-inch baking dish with butter-flavored cooking spray. In a large skillet sprayed with butter-flavored cooking spray, brown chicken pieces for 3 to 4 minutes on each side. In a large bowl, combine toast cubes, celery, and onion. Add ½ cup chicken soup, water, sage, and black pepper. Mix well to combine. Pat mixture evenly into prepared baking dish. Evenly arrange browned chicken pieces over dressing mixture. Drizzle remaining chicken soup evenly over top. Cover and bake for 30 minutes. Uncover and continue baking for 15 minutes or until vegetables and chicken are tender. Divide into 4 servings.

Each serving equals:

HE: 3 Protein • 1 Bread • ¾ Vegetable • ½ Slider •
5 Optional Calories

---

269 Calories • 5 gm Fat • 30 gm Protein •
26 gm Carbohydrate • 536 mg Sodium •
65 mg Calcium • 1 gm Fiber

DIABETIC EXCHANGES: 3 Meat • 1 Starch •
½ Vegetable • ½ Other Carbohydrate

Ice Cream Cake Roll

⟳ Serves 8

4 eggs, separated
¾ cup Splenda Granular☆
1 teaspoon vanilla extract
¾ cup cake flour
1 teaspoon baking powder
¼ teaspoon baking soda
3 cups Wells' Blue Bunny sugar- and fat-free chocolate ice cream
*   or any sugar- and fat-free ice cream*

Preheat oven to 375 degrees. Line a 15½-inch-by-10½-inch-by-1-inch jelly roll pan with waxed paper. Lightly spray paper with butter-flavored cooking spray. In a large bowl, beat egg yolks with a wire whisk until thick and lemon colored. Stir in ¼ cup Splenda and vanilla extract. In another large bowl, beat egg whites with an electric mixer on HIGH until soft peaks form. Add remaining ½ cup Splenda and continue beating on HIGH until stiff peaks form. Using a wire whisk, fold egg yolks into beaten egg whites. Add flour, baking powder, and baking soda. Mix gently using a wire whisk. Evenly spread batter in prepared jelly roll pan. Bake for 12 minutes or until a toothpick inserted in center comes out clean. DO NOT OVERBAKE. Loosen sides, then turn out on a clean towel. Peel off waxed paper. Starting at narrow end, roll cake and towel together. Cool on a wire rack. When cooled, carefully unroll and remove towel. In a medium bowl, stir ice cream with a sturdy spoon just until soft. Spread softened ice cream over cake. Roll up. Wrap in aluminum foil and freeze for at least 2 hours. Just before serving, cut into 8 (2-inch) even slices.

Each serving equals:

HE: ½ Bread • ½ Protein • ¾ Slider •
9 Optional Calories

---

150 Calories • 2 gm Fat • 7 gm Protein •
26 gm Carbohydrate • 159 mg Sodium •
138 mg Calcium • 0 gm Fiber

DIABETIC EXCHANGES: ½ Starch • ½ Meat •
½ Other Carbohydrate

Sweet Summer Supper

I'd serve this meal for a summer birthday or even on the Fourth of July, if you weren't having a cookout! It's got all the things that make summer special, from the vivid colors and juicy joys of fresh melon to the spectacular flavor of fresh strawberries and ice cream on a hot, starlit evening. It's not too filling, so you can even go for a swim an hour later—or just relax under the full moon and breathe the balmy night air.

THE PLAN: This splendid summer menu begins with the making of meringues for the **Strawberry Ice Cream Meringues**, which require an hour in the oven to bake PLUS an hour to rest and set. So choose this meal on a night when you've got a bit of extra time to make it special. Next, you can make your **Melon Salad** and **Supper Chicken Salad**; both improve with a half hour in the refrigerator. With less than 30 minutes to go, bake your **Bacon Corn Muffins**, which are best served warm. Who needs fireworks when you've got such a scrumptious supper?

Melon Salad

● Serves 6 (1 cup)

3 cups diced ripe cantaloupe
1½ cups diced ripe watermelon
1½ cups diced honeydew melon
¼ cup Diet Mountain Dew

In a large bowl, combine cantaloupe, watermelon, and honeydew melon. Drizzle Diet Mountain Dew over top. Gently stir to combine. Cover and refrigerate for at least 30 minutes. Gently stir again just before serving.

Each serving equals:

HE: 1 Fruit

---

56 Calories • 0 gm Fat • 1 gm Protein •
13 gm Carbohydrate • 13 mg Sodium •
14 mg Calcium • 1 gm Fiber

DIABETIC EXCHANGES: 1 Fruit

Supper Chicken Salad

○ Serves 6 (1 cup)

  2 full cups diced cooked chicken breast
  1½ cups chopped celery
  1½ cups seedless green grapes
  ¾ cup Kraft fat-free mayonnaise
  2 tablespoons lemon juice
  2 hard-boiled eggs, chopped
  ¼ cup slivered almonds, toasted

In a large bowl, combine chicken, celery, and grapes. Add mayonnaise and lemon juice. Mix well to combine. Fold in chopped eggs and almonds. Cover and refrigerate for at least 30 minutes. Gently stir again just before serving.

HINTS: 1. If you don't have leftovers, purchase a chunk of cooked chicken breast from your local deli.
2. To toast almonds, spread in a glass pie plate and microwave on HIGH (100 percent power) for 6 to 7 minutes or until golden. Stir after 3 minutes; then each minute thereafter until done.

Each serving equals:

HE: 2½ Protein • ½ Fruit • ½ Vegetable • ⅓ Fat • ¼ Slider

---

199 Calories • 7 gm Fat • 21 gm Protein • 13 gm Carbohydrate • 330 mg Sodium • 47 mg Calcium • 2 gm Fiber

---

DIABETIC EXCHANGES: 2½ Meat • ½ Fruit • ½ Fat

Bacon Corn Muffins

● Serves 6

½ cup + 1 tablespoon all-purpose flour

½ cup yellow cornmeal

2 tablespoons Splenda Granular

2 teaspoons baking powder

¼ teaspoon table salt

½ cup fat-free milk

1 egg or equivalent in egg substitute

2 tablespoons vegetable oil

6 tablespoons Oscar Mayer or Hormel Real Bacon Bits

Preheat oven to 425 degrees. Spray 6 wells of a 12-hole muffin pan with butter-flavored cooking spray or line with paper liners. In a large bowl, combine flour, cornmeal, Splenda, baking powder, and salt. In a small bowl, combine milk, egg, and vegetable oil. Add milk mixture to flour mixture. Mix gently just to combine. Fold in bacon bits. Fill prepared muffin wells ⅔ full. Bake for 12 to 15 minutes. Place muffin pan on a wire rack and let set 5 minutes. Serve warm.

HINT: Fill unused muffin wells with water. It protects the muffin pan and ensures even baking.

Each serving equals:

HE: 1¼ Bread • 1 Fat • ½ Slider • 5 Optional Calories

175 Calories • 7 gm Fat • 7 gm Protein •
21 gm Carbohydrate • 501 mg Sodium •
122 mg Calcium • 1 gm Fiber

DIABETIC EXCHANGES: 1 Starch • 1 Fat • ½ Meat

Strawberry Ice Cream Meringues

○ Serves 6

6 egg whites
1 cup Splenda Granular
¼ teaspoon cream of tartar
1 teaspoon vanilla extract
3 cups Wells' Blue Bunny sugar- and fat-free strawberry
*   ice cream or any sugar- and fat-free ice cream*
3 cups sliced fresh strawberries

Preheat oven to 275 degrees. Cover a large baking sheet with waxed paper. In a large glass bowl, beat egg whites with an electric mixer on HIGH until soft peaks form. Add Splenda, cream of tartar, and vanilla extract. Continue beating on HIGH until stiff peaks form. Form into 6 large meringue shells on waxed paper, using about ¾ cup mixture for each. Shape with a spoon to form shells. Bake for 1 hour. Turn heat off and let meringues set in oven, with the door closed, for another hour. When ready to serve, spoon about ½ cup ice cream in center of each shell and top with ½ cup strawberries.

Each serving equals:

HE: ½ Fat Free Milk • ½ Fruit • ⅓ Protein •
½ Slider • 11 Optional Calories

140 Calories • 0 gm Fat • 8 gm Protein •
27 gm Carbohydrate • 105 mg Sodium •
133 mg Calcium • 2 gm Fiber

DIABETIC EXCHANGES: 1 Other Carbohydrate •
½ Fruit • ½ Meat

A Creamy, Dreamy Dinner

It's luscious with a capital L, this downright delectable dinner that will fulfill every fantasy you've ever had about creamy dishes at every course! In fact, it's likely that no one will believe this meal is part of a healthy diet, thanks to those brilliant creators of great-tasting fat-free products who help it to be possible.

THE PLAN: Start making culinary magic by mixing up **Decadent Chocolate Cream Pie.** (Just the name sounds outrageous, doesn't it?) That needs to chill for an hour. I'd suggest making the **Cream of Carrot Soup** next, which requires a bit of blending to make it extra-creamy. You've never tasted creaminess and crunchiness all at once, as in my **Sour Cream Coleslaw**, which you'll stir up and then refrigerate. The entrée is a quick one, a simple skillet preparation, but everyone who tastes this **Chicken and Peas Tetrazzini** will be dazzled by its scrumptious texture and flavor. After this meal, you're bound to enjoy sweet dreams!

Sour Cream Coleslaw

● Serves 6 (1 cup)

¾ cup Land O Lakes no-fat sour cream
⅓ cup Kraft fat-free mayonnaise
1 tablespoon Splenda Granular
1 tablespoon prepared yellow mustard
⅛ teaspoon black pepper
1½ teaspoons dried parsley flakes
6 cups shredded cabbage
½ cup finely shredded carrots
¼ cup finely chopped onion

In a large bowl, combine sour cream, mayonnaise, Splenda, mustard, black pepper, and parsley flakes. Add cabbage, carrots, and onion. Mix well to combine. Cover and refrigerate for at least 30 minutes. Gently stir again just before serving.

Each serving equals:

HE: 1¼ Vegetable • ¼ Slider • 19 Optional Calories

60 Calories • 0 gm Fat • 2 gm Protein •
13 gm Carbohydrate • 193 mg Sodium •
88 mg Calcium • 3 gm Fiber

DIABETIC EXCHANGES: 1 Vegetable • ½ Carbohydrate

Cream of Carrot Soup

⊙ Serves 6 (1 cup)

1 cup chopped onion
2 (14-ounce) cans Swanson Lower Sodium Fat Free
Chicken Broth
5 cups diced carrots
½ teaspoon lemon pepper
1½ teaspoons dried parsley flakes
2 cups Carnation Nonfat Dry Milk Powder
1½ cups water

In a medium saucepan sprayed with butter-flavored cooking spray, sauté onion for 5 minutes or until tender. Add chicken broth, carrots, lemon pepper, and parsley flakes. Cook over medium heat for 15 to 20 minutes or until carrots are soft. Reserve about ⅓ cup of cooked mixture. Pour remaining vegetables and broth into a blender container. Cover and process on BLEND for 15 to 20 seconds or until mixture is smooth. Pour mixture back into saucepan. In a small bowl, combine dry milk powder and water. Stir milk mixture and reserved ⅓ cup vegetable mixture into saucepan. Continue cooking for 5 minutes or until heated through, stirring often.

Each serving equals:

HE: 2 Vegetable • 1 Fat Free Milk •
10 Optional Calories

144 Calories • 0 gm Fat • 11 gm Protein •
25 gm Carbohydrate • 301 mg Sodium •
338 mg Calcium • 3 gm Fiber

DIABETIC EXCHANGES: 2 Vegetable • 1 Fat Free Milk

Chicken and Peas Tetrazzini

● Serves 6 (1 cup)

> ¾ *cup chopped onion*
> *1 (10¾-ounce) can Healthy Request Cream of Chicken Soup*
> *1 cup fat-free milk*
> ¼ *cup Kraft Reduced Fat Parmesan Style Grated Topping*
> ⅛ *teaspoon black pepper*
> 1½ *teaspoons dried parsley flakes*
> *1 cup frozen peas, thawed*
> *1 (2-ounce) jar chopped pimiento, drained*
> *2 cups cooked spaghetti, rinsed and drained*
> 1½ *cups diced cooked chicken breast*

In a large skillet sprayed with butter-flavored cooking spray, sauté onion for 5 minutes. Stir in chicken soup, milk, Parmesan cheese, black pepper, and parsley flakes. Add peas, pimiento, spaghetti, and chicken. Mix well to combine. Lower heat and simmer for 6 to 8 minutes, stirring occasionally.

HINTS: 1. Thaw peas by placing in a colander and rinsing under hot water for 1 minute.
2. Usually 1½ cups uncooked broken spaghetti cooks to about 2 cups.
3. If you don't have leftovers, purchase a chunk of cooked chicken breast from your local deli.

Each serving equals:

HE: 1½ Protein • 1 Bread • ¼ Vegetable • ½ Slider • 5 Optional Calories

216 Calories • 4 gm Fat • 18 gm Protein • 27 gm Carbohydrate • 308 mg Sodium • 93 mg Calcium • 2 gm Fiber

DIABETIC EXCHANGES: 1½ Meat • 1½ Starch • ½ Other Carbohydrate

Decadent Chocolate Cream Pie

○ Serves 8

> 2 (4-serving) packages JELL-O sugar-free instant chocolate
>   pudding mix
> 1⅓ cups Carnation Nonfat Dry Milk Powder
> 2½ cups water
> 1 (6-ounce) Keebler chocolate pie crust
> 6 (2½-inch) chocolate graham cracker squares, made into
>   fine crumbs
> 1½ cups Cool Whip Free☆
> 1 tablespoon Hershey's Lite Chocolate Syrup

In a large bowl, combine chocolate pudding mixes, dry milk powder, and water. Mix well using a wire whisk. Evenly spread pudding mixture into pie crust. Refrigerate while preparing next layer. In a small bowl, gently combine chocolate graham cracker crumbs and 1 cup Cool Whip Free. Evenly spread mixture over set filling. In a small bowl, gently combine remaining ½ cup Cool Whip Free and chocolate syrup. Spread topping mixture evenly over top. Refrigerate for at least 1 hour. Cut into 8 servings.

HINT: A self-seal sandwich bag works great for crushing graham
    crackers.

Each serving equals:

HE: 1¼ Bread • ½ Fat Free Milk • ½ Fat •
½ Slider • 18 Optional Calories

218 Calories • 6 gm Fat • 7 gm Protein •
34 gm Carbohydrate • 480 mg Sodium •
151 mg Calcium • 1 gm Fiber

DIABETIC EXCHANGES: 1 Starch • ½ Fat Free Milk •
½ Fat • ½ Other Carbohydrate

A Chicken in Every Pot

It's a slogan good enough to get a President elected and keep him in office for years—and it's a great way to feed your family, too! In this case, the "chicken" is a fantastically good pot pie made with a special twist. But it's only the main event; you've got a spectacular dessert to offer your family or guests, and an old-fashioned fizzy drink that will bring back memories or make new ones.

THE PLAN: I'm going to suggest you bake first, since **Orange Cake with Lemon Cream Sauce** needs to cool completely before you cover it with a delectable creamy-sweet sauce that you'll prepare while the cake is in the oven. Once it's set on a rack to cool, you can get going on your **Cheesy Chicken Pot Pie**, which requires a slightly warmer oven. You'll whip up **Lettuce Salad with Cucumber Dill Dressing** and **Vanilla Sodas** right before everyone sits down. This is a meal that could surely get you elected to office!

Lettuce Salad with Cucumber Dill Dressing

○ Serves 6

6 tablespoons Kraft Fat Free Ranch Dressing
2 tablespoons Kraft fat-free mayonnaise
1 cup peeled and finely chopped cucumber
½ teaspoon dried dill weed
6 cups shredded lettuce

In a blender container, combine ranch dressing, mayonnaise, and cucumber. Cover and process on BLEND for 10 seconds or until mixture is smooth. Scrape mixture into a small bowl. Stir in dill weed. For each salad, place 1 cup lettuce on a salad plate and drizzle a full 3 tablespoons dressing mixture over top. Serve at once.

Each serving equals:

HE: 1 Vegetable • ¼ Slider • 6 Optional Calories

40 Calories • 0 gm Fat • 1 gm Protein •
9 gm Carbohydrate • 261 mg Sodium •
21 mg Calcium • 1 gm Fiber

DIABETIC EXCHANGES: 1 Vegetable

Cheesy Chicken Pot Pie

⊙ Serves 6

> 1 (10¾-ounce) can Healthy Request Cream of Chicken
>   Soup
> ½ cup fat-free milk
> ¾ cup cubed Velveeta Light processed cheese
> 1 (16-ounce) package frozen broccoli, cauliflower and
>   carrot blend, thawed
> 2 full cups diced cooked chicken breast
> 1 (7.5-ounce) can Pillsbury refrigerated buttermilk biscuits
> Paprika

Preheat oven to 400 degrees. Spray an 8-by-8-inch baking dish with butter-flavored cooking spray. In a large skillet sprayed with butter-flavored cooking spray, combine chicken soup, milk, and Velveeta cheese. Add thawed vegetables and chicken. Mix well to combine. Cook over medium heat for 6 minutes or until cheese melts and mixture is heated through, stirring often. Spoon hot mixture into prepared baking dish. Bake for 15 minutes. Meanwhile, separate biscuits and cut each into quarters. Sprinkle biscuit pieces over partially baked chicken mixture. Spray tops of biscuit pieces with butter-flavored cooking spray. Lightly sprinkle paprika over top. Continue baking for 15 minutes or until biscuits are golden brown. Place baking dish on a wire rack and let set for 5 minutes. Divide into 6 servings.

HINTS: 1. Thaw vegetables by placing in a colander and rinsing under hot water for 1 minute.
2. If you don't have leftovers, purchase a chunk of cooked chicken breast from your local deli.

Each serving equals:

HE: 2½ Protein • 1¼ Bread • ½ Vegetable •
¼ Slider • 19 Optional Calories

261 Calories • 5 gm Fat • 26 gm Protein •
28 gm Carbohydrate • 681 mg Sodium •
141 mg Calcium • 2 gm Fiber

DIABETIC EXCHANGES: 2½ Meat • 1½ Starch •
½ Vegetable

Orange Cake with Lemon Cream Sauce

◐ Serves 8

1½ cups Bisquick Reduced Fat Baking Mix
1 teaspoon baking powder
¾ cup Splenda Granular
1 cup unsweetened orange juice
2 eggs or equivalent in egg substitute
¼ cup I Can't Believe It's Not Butter! Light Margarine
1 (11-ounce) can mandarin oranges, rinsed and drained
1 (4-serving) package JELL-O sugar-free vanilla cook-and-serve
    pudding mix
1 (4-serving) package JELL-O sugar-free lemon gelatin
1½ cups Diet Mountain Dew
½ cup Cool Whip Free

Preheat oven to 350 degrees. Spray a 9-inch round cake pan with butter-flavored cooking spray. In a large bowl, combine baking mix, baking powder, and Splenda. Add orange juice, eggs, and margarine. Mix gently just to combine. Gently fold in mandarin oranges. Spread batter into prepared pan. Bake for 25 to 30 minutes or until cake tests done in center. Meanwhile, in a medium saucepan, combine dry pudding mix, dry gelatin, and Diet Mountain Dew. Cook over medium heat until mixture thickens and starts to boil, stirring often. Remove from heat and place saucepan on a wire rack to cool, stirring occasionally. When cake is through baking, place pan on a wire rack and allow cake to cool completely. After both cake and sauce are cooled, gently fold Cool Whip Free into lemon sauce. Carefully spread sauce mixture over cooled cake. Cut into 8 wedges. Refrigerate leftovers.

Each serving equals:

HE: 1 Bread • ¾ Fat • ½ Fruit • ¼ Protein •
¼ Slider • 11 Optional Calories

185 Calories • 5 gm Fat • 5 gm Protein •
30 gm Carbohydrate • 403 mg Sodium •
66 mg Calcium • 1 gm Fiber

DIABETIC EXCHANGES: 1 Starch • 1 Fat • ½ Fruit •
½ Other Carbohydrate

Vanilla Sodas

○ Serves 6 (1 cup)

3 cups cold club soda
3 cups Wells' Blue Bunny sugar- and fat-free vanilla ice cream
or any sugar- and fat-free ice cream

In a blender container, combine 1½ cups club soda and 1½ cups ice cream. Cover and process on BLEND for 15 to 20 seconds or until mixture is smooth. Evenly pour into 3 glasses. Repeat with remaining club soda and ice cream. Serve at once.

Each serving equals:

HE: 1 Slider

---

80 Calories • 0 gm Fat • 4 gm Protein •
16 gm Carbohydrate • 75 mg Sodium •
126 mg Calcium • 0 gm Fiber

DIABETIC EXCHANGES: 1 Other Carbohydrate

Treat Yourself to Turkey

Most of us end up with extra turkey during the holidays and always need good ideas for those eternal leftovers. But you can also purchase reasonably priced whole turkey breasts year-round and make this healthy poultry a more frequent feature on your menu.

THE PLAN: Do you come from a family that always serves a molded gelatin salad on festive occasions? If you do, then you know you'll start this menu by making **Molded Cranberry Waldorf Salad**, a rosy-red and tangy treat that must be refrigerated for a few hours before served. Next, you'll be baking up a fragrant storm with **Sour Cream Nutmeg Cake**, a luscious creamy treat of a dessert that everyone will love. You'll need two skillets to prepare your veggie dish (**Apricot Glazed Carrots**—mmm-good!) and a delightfully crunchy **Turkey Chow Mein.** I'd probably do the carrots first and just keep them warm while I finish up the turkey dish. After you've tried this menu, you might decide to buy an even larger turkey than usual this year!

Molded Cranberry Waldorf Salad

○ Serves 6

2 cups Ocean Spray reduced-calorie cranberry juice cocktail☆
1 (4-serving) package JELL-O sugar-free lemon gelatin
1 cup (2 small) cored, unpeeled, and chopped
   Red Delicious apples
¾ cup chopped celery
¼ cup chopped walnuts
6 lettuce leaves
6 tablespoons Kraft fat-free mayonnaise

In a medium saucepan, bring 1 cup cranberry juice cocktail to a boil. Remove from heat. Add dry gelatin. Mix well to dissolve gelatin. Stir in remaining 1 cup cranberry juice cocktail. Add apples, celery, and walnuts. Mix well to combine. Pour mixture into an 8-by-8-inch dish. Refrigerate until firm, about 3 hours. Cut into 6 pieces. For each serving, place a lettuce leaf on a salad plate, arrange a piece of salad over lettuce, and top with 1 tablespoon mayonnaise.

Each serving equals:

HE: ⅔ Fruit • ⅓ Fat • ¼ Vegetable •
16 Optional Calories

---

71 Calories • 3 gm Fat • 1 gm Protein •
10 gm Carbohydrate • 139 mg Sodium •
20 mg Calcium • 1 gm Fiber

DIABETIC EXCHANGES: 1 Fruit • ½ Fat

Apricot Glazed Carrots

● Serves 6 (scant ½ cup)

> *3 tablespoons apricot spreadable fruit*
> *¼ cup Splenda Granular*
> *1 teaspoon dried parsley flakes*
> *3 cups frozen sliced carrots, thawed*
> *2 tablespoons I Can't Believe It's Not Butter! Light Margarine*

In a medium skillet sprayed with butter-flavored cooking spray, combine spreadable fruit, Splenda, and parsley flakes. Stir in carrots. Add margarine. Mix gently to combine. Cover and cook over low heat for 10 to 12 minutes or until mixture is heated through and carrots are tender, stirring often.

HINT: Thaw carrots by placing in a colander and rinsing under hot water for 1 minute.

Each serving equals:

HE: 1 Vegetable • ½ Fruit • ½ Fat • 4 Optional Calories

---

66 Calories • 2 gm Fat • 1 gm Protein •
11 gm Carbohydrate • 83 mg Sodium •
22 mg Calcium • 2 gm Fiber

DIABETIC EXCHANGES: 1 Vegetable • ½ Fruit • ½ Fat

Turkey Chow Mein

○ Serves 6

½ cup chopped onion

1 cup sliced celery

½ cup chopped green bell pepper

*1 (4-ounce) jar sliced mushrooms, drained and ¼ cup liquid
    reserved*

2 full cups diced cooked turkey breast

*1 (10¾-ounce) can Healthy Request Cream of Chicken
    Soup*

2 tablespoons reduced-sodium soy sauce

3 cups hot cooked rice

6 tablespoons coarsely chopped chow mein noodles

In a large skillet sprayed with butter-flavored cooking spray, sauté onion, celery, and green pepper for 6 to 8 minutes. Stir in mushrooms and turkey. Add chicken soup, reserved mushroom liquid, and soy sauce. Mix well to combine. Continue cooking for 5 to 6 minutes or until mixture is heated through, stirring occasionally. For each serving, place ½ cup rice on a plate, spoon about ½ cup turkey mixture over rice, and sprinkle 2 tablespoons chow mein noodles over top.

HINTS: 1. If you don't have leftovers, purchase a chunk of cooked turkey breast from your local deli.
2. Usually 2 cups uncooked instant rice cooks to about 3 cups.
3. 1 cup drained bean sprouts may be added, if desired.

Each serving equals:

HE: 2 Protein • 1½ Bread • 1 Vegetable • ¼ Slider •
13 Optional Calories

---

223 Calories • 3 gm Fat • 21 gm Protein •
28 gm Carbohydrate • 509 mg Sodium •
29 mg Calcium • 2 gm Fiber

DIABETIC EXCHANGES: 2 Meat • 1½ Starch •
½ Vegetable • ½ Other Carbohydrate

Sour Cream Nutmeg Cake

⬤ Serves 8

¾ cup Land O Lakes no-fat sour cream
½ teaspoon baking soda
1½ cups Splenda Granular
1½ cups cake flour
⅓ cup I Can't Believe It's Not Butter! Light Margarine
1 egg or equivalent in egg substitute
¾ teaspoon ground nutmeg
½ cup Cool Whip Lite

Preheat oven to 350 degrees. Spray an 8-inch round cake pan with butter-flavored cooking spray. In a small bowl, combine sour cream and baking soda. Set aside. In a large bowl, combine Splenda, flour, and margarine. Mix well using a pastry blender until mixture is crumbly. Pat half of mixture into prepared pan. Add sour cream mixture, egg, and nutmeg to remaining flour mixture. Mix gently just to combine. Spoon batter evenly over crumb mixture. Bake for 20 to 25 minutes or until a toothpick inserted in center comes out clean. Place pan on a wire rack and let set for at least 10 minutes. Cut into 8 wedges. When serving, top each piece with 1 tablespoon Cool Whip Lite.

Each serving equals:

HE: 1 Bread • 1 Fat • ½ Slider • 19 Optional Calories

157 Calories • 5 gm Fat • 3 gm Protein •
25 gm Carbohydrate • 207 mg Sodium •
38 mg Calcium • 1 gm Fiber

DIABETIC EXCHANGES: 1 Starch • 1 Fat •
½ Other Carbohydrate

Beef

Cozy "Fireside" Family Dinner

If you've got an old-fashioned fireplace in your family room, per-haps you'd like to serve this menu there while everyone shares news of the day. But even if you haven't got your very own "fire-side," I offer this cozy meal as a way to feel that same kind of warmth as you and your family dine.

THE PLAN: Once you start baking my **Johnny Appleseed Bars**, your kids are sure to poke their heads in to check on dinner—they smell *that* good! After you get dessert going, it's time to make my **Hearty Chili**, a simple but spectacularly good version of this fam-ily favorite. While it's simmering, chop up the ingredients for a **Crisp Relish Salad**, and then mix up some **Hot "Cider."** While the bars cool, you'll be serving a scrumptious supper, with a heart-warming treat to follow.

Crisp Relish Salad

● Serves 4

> 1 cup grated carrots
> ½ cup finely chopped celery
> ¼ cup finely chopped green onion
> ¼ cup finely chopped red radishes
> ¼ cup Kraft Fat Free Catalina Dressing
> 4 lettuce leaves

In a medium bowl, combine carrots, celery, green onion, and radishes. Add Catalina dressing. Mix well to combine. Cover and refrigerate for at least 15 minutes. When serving, place 1 lettuce leaf on a salad plate and spoon about ½ cup salad mixture over top.

Each serving equals:

HE: 1 Vegetable • 17 Optional Calories

32 Calories • 0 gm Fat • 0 gm Protein •
8 gm Carbohydrate • 186 mg Sodium •
16 mg Calcium • 2 gm Fiber

DIABETIC EXCHANGES: 1 Vegetable

Hearty Chili

○ Serves 4 (1½ cups)

> *8 ounces extra-lean ground sirloin beef or turkey breast*
> *1 cup chopped onion*
> *1 (8-ounce) can Hunt's Tomato Sauce*
> *1 (15-ounce) can diced tomatoes, undrained*
> *½ cup water*
> *1 teaspoon chili seasoning*
> *1 (15-ounce) can pinto beans, rinsed and drained*
> *1 (8-ounce) can cut green beans, rinsed and drained*

In a medium saucepan sprayed with butter-flavored cooking spray, brown meat and onion. Stir in tomato sauce, undrained tomatoes, water, and chili seasoning. Add pinto beans and green beans. Mix well to combine. Lower heat and simmer for 10 minutes, stirring occasionally.

HINT: For those who like their chili sweet, add 1 tablespoon Splenda when adding tomatoes.

Each serving equals:

HE: 3 Vegetable • 2½ Protein • ½ Bread

---

196 Calories • 4 gm Fat • 16 gm Protein •
24 gm Carbohydrate • 780 mg Sodium •
73 mg Calcium • 7 gm Fiber

DIABETIC EXCHANGES: 3 Vegetable • 2 Meat • 1 Starch

Johnny Appleseed Bars

⊙ Serves 8 (3 each)

> 1 cup Musselman's "No Sugar Added" Applesauce
> ¼ cup I Can't Believe It's Not Butter! Light Margarine
> 2 tablespoons fat-free milk
> 1 cup + 2 tablespoons Bisquick Reduced Fat Baking Mix
> ¾ cup Splenda Granular
> 1 teaspoon baking powder
> 1½ teaspoons apple pie spice
> ¼ cup chopped walnuts
> ¾ cup seedless raisins

Preheat oven to 350 degrees. Spray an 8-by-8-inch cake pan with butter-flavored cooking spray. In a medium saucepan, combine applesauce and margarine. Cook over medium heat until margarine melts, stirring often. Remove from heat. Stir in milk. Add baking mix, Splenda, baking powder, and apple pie spice. Mix just to combine. Fold in walnuts and raisins. Spread batter evenly into prepared pan. Bake for 25 to 30 minutes or until top springs back in center when lightly touched. Place pan on a wire rack and let set for at least 5 minutes. Cut into 24 bars.

HINT: Good warm or cold. Also good topped with Cool Whip Lite. If using, count the additional calories accordingly.

Each serving equals:

HE: 1 Fruit • 1 Fat • ¾ Bread • 18 Optional Calories

---

200 Calories • 8 gm Fat • 3 gm Protein •
29 gm Carbohydrate • 397 mg Sodium •
73 mg Calcium • 2 gm Fiber

DIABETIC EXCHANGES: 1 Fruit • 1 Fat • 1 Starch

Hot "Cider"

❂ Serves 4 (¾ cup)

2 cups unsweetened apple juice
1 cup Diet Mountain Dew
2 tablespoons Splenda Granular
½ teaspoon apple pie spice

In a medium saucepan, combine apple juice and Diet Mountain Dew. Stir in Splenda and apple pie spice. Cook over medium heat for 5 minutes or until hot, stirring occasionally. Serve at once.

Each serving equals:

HE: 1 Fruit • 3 Optional Calories

60 Calories • 0 gm Fat • 0 gm Protein •
15 gm Carbohydrate • 9 mg Sodium • 9 mg Calcium •
0 gm Fiber

DIABETIC EXCHANGES: 1 Fruit

Cowboy Cookin'

If you've ever worked outside for hours, you know just how hungry you can get! My theme for this menu is the American cowboy (or cowgirl, of course) who depends on the camp cook for the kind of substantial fare that provides energy for a very active life. We all need that kind of energy these days, with our busy schedules, and so here's a menu to please the palate and fill you up!

THE PLAN: This is a very quickly prepared meal, good for evenings when you've got a book club meeting or want to get a head start on closet cleaning before your favorite TV show. You've got two make-ahead dishes that can chill while you make the others. **Butter-scotch-Apricot Pudding Treats** offer a delightful combo of flavors, and my **Dilly Cucumbers** are sure to become a family favorite all summer long. **Skillet Green Beans and Mushrooms** need little attention as they simmer away on the stove, and so you can focus on **Cowboy Spaghetti**, a fun and filling recipe that calls for cooked spaghetti, so be sure to get it ready before you start this dish. (I recommend keeping cooked pasta in the fridge for just such quick dishes as this one. Take out what you need and reheat it in the microwave while you're browning the meat!) Whether you've got a home on the range or an apartment in the city, you'll be a fan of cowboy cooking, wait and see!

Dilly Cucumbers

⏾ Serves 4 (½ cup)

½ cup Land O Lakes no-fat sour cream
1 tablespoon Land O Lakes Fat Free Half & Half
2 tablespoons Splenda Granular
1 teaspoon dried dill weed
⅛ teaspoon black pepper
½ cup finely chopped onion
2½ cups thinly sliced peeled cucumbers

In a medium bowl, combine sour cream, half & half, Splenda, dill weed, and black pepper. Add onion and cucumbers. Mix gently to combine. Cover and refrigerate for at least 20 minutes. Gently stir again just before serving.

Each serving equals:

HE: 1½ Vegetable • ¼ Slider • 15 Optional Calories

48 Calories • 0 gm Fat • 2 gm Protein •
10 gm Carbohydrate • 46 mg Sodium •
65 mg Calcium • 1 gm Fiber

DIABETIC EXCHANGES: 1 Vegetable •
½ Other Carbohydrate

Skillet Green Beans and Mushrooms

● Serves 4 (¾ cup)

3 cups frozen cut green beans, thawed
1 (10¾-ounce) can Healthy Request Cream of Mushroom Soup
2 tablespoons Land O Lakes Fat Free Half & Half
1 (4-ounce) jar sliced mushrooms, drained
2 teaspoons I Can't Believe It's Not Butter! Light Margarine
2 teaspoons dried onion flakes
⅛ teaspoon black pepper

In a large skillet sprayed with butter-flavored cooking spray, sauté green beans for 5 minutes. Stir in mushroom soup and half & half. Add mushrooms, margarine, onion flakes, and black pepper. Mix well to combine. Lower heat and simmer for 8 to 10 minutes or until mixture is heated through, stirring often.

Each serving equals:

HE: 2 Vegetable • ¼ Fat • ½ Slider •
6 Optional Calories

103 Calories • 3 gm Fat • 3 gm Protein •
16 gm Carbohydrate • 493 mg Sodium •
119 mg Calcium • 3 gm Fiber

DIABETIC EXCHANGES: 2 Vegetable •
½ Other Carbohydrate

Cowboy Spaghetti

● Serves 4 (1 cup)

8 ounces extra-lean ground sirloin beef or turkey breast
½ cup finely chopped onion
1 (10¾-ounce) can Healthy Request Tomato Soup
1 cup chunky salsa (mild, medium, or hot)
½ cup water
1½ cups cooked spaghetti, rinsed and drained
¼ cup chopped ripe olives
¾ cup shredded Kraft reduced-fat Cheddar cheese
1 teaspoon dried parsley flakes
⅛ teaspoon black pepper

In a large skillet sprayed with butter-flavored cooking spray, brown meat and onion. Stir in tomato soup, salsa, and water. Add spaghetti, olives, Cheddar cheese, parsley flakes, and black pepper. Mix well to combine. Lower heat and simmer for 6 to 8 minutes or until mixture is heated through, stirring often.

HINT: Usually 1 cup broken uncooked spaghetti cooks to about 1½ cups.

Each serving equals:

HE: 2½ Protein • ¾ Bread • ¾ Vegetable • ¼ Fat •
½ Slider • 5 Optional Calories

296 Calories • 8 gm Fat • 22 gm Protein •
34 gm Carbohydrate • 896 mg Sodium •
155 mg Calcium • 4 gm Fiber

DIABETIC EXCHANGES: 2 Meat • 1 Starch •
1 Vegetable • ½ Other Carbohydrate

Butterscotch-Apricot Pudding Treats

● Serves 4

1 (15-ounce) can apricots, packed in fruit juice, undrained

2 tablespoons water

1 (4-serving) package JELL-O sugar-free instant butterscotch pudding mix

⅔ cup Carnation Nonfat Dry Milk Powder

½ cup Cool Whip Lite☆

2 tablespoons chopped walnuts

In a blender container, combine undrained apricots and water. Cover and process on BLEND for 10 to 15 seconds or until mixture is smooth. In a large bowl, combine dry pudding mix and dry milk powder. Add blended apricot mixture. Mix well using a wire whisk. Blend in ¼ cup Cool Whip Lite and walnuts. Evenly spoon mixture into 4 dessert dishes. Top each with 1 tablespoon Cool Whip Lite. Refrigerate for at least 15 minutes.

Each serving equals:

HE: 1 Fruit • ½ Fat Free Milk • ¼ Fat • ½ Slider • 13 Optional Calories

163 Calories • 3 gm Fat • 5 gm Protein • 29 gm Carbohydrate • 367 mg Sodium • 168 mg Calcium • 2 gm Fiber

DIABETIC EXCHANGES: 1 Fruit • ½ Fat Free Milk • ½ Other Carbohydrate

Cooking with Cliff

My husband leaves most of the cooking to me and always has, but he's been my constant and most appreciative fan. I always joke he'll eat almost anything but broccoli, and it's true, as long as the dishes I serve are genuinely tasty. When I began cooking the Healthy Exchanges Way all those years ago, I said farewell to "diet slop" forever. By learning to satisfy Cliff's appetite, I developed recipes that would please just about everyone—and help them eat healthy for the rest of their lives.

THE PLAN: Like most men, Cliff loves cheesecake, and **Majestic Cheesecake Tarts** are like little chocolate cheesecakes topped with nuts, chips, and coconut—yum! These scored a perfect 10 with Cliff and my grandsons. Make these first and refrigerate until serving. Next, stir up a crunchy **Waldorf Apple Salad** and let it chill. Now for the manly main dish: **Cliff's Ground Beef and Macaroni**, a skillet pleaser that will simmer on your stovetop until it's done. Serve this meal with a glass of **Sparkling Orange Spritzer**, and you're sure to win your family's award for Favorite Chef!

Waldorf Apple Salad

○ Serves 6 (¾ cup)

⅓ cup Kraft fat-free mayonnaise

1 tablespoon Splenda Granular

1 teaspoon lemon juice

½ cup Cool Whip Free

3 cups (6 small) cored, unpeeled, and diced Red Delicious
apples

1½ cups diced celery

¼ cup chopped walnuts

In a large bowl, combine mayonnaise, Splenda, and lemon juice. Stir in Cool Whip Free. Add apples, celery, and walnuts. Mix gently to combine. Cover and refrigerate for at least 15 minutes. Gently stir again just before serving.

Each serving equals:

HE: 1 Fruit • ½ Vegetable • ⅓ Fat • ¼ Slider •
13 Optional Calories

87 Calories • 3 gm Fat • 1 gm Protein •
14 gm Carbohydrate • 130 mg Sodium •
21 mg Calcium • 2 gm Fiber

DIABETIC EXCHANGES: 1 Fruit • ½ Vegetable • ½ Fat

Cliff's Ground Beef and Macaroni

○ Serves 6 (1¼ cups)

16 ounces extra-lean ground sirloin beef or turkey breast
½ cup chopped onion
1 (14-ounce) can Swanson Lower Sodium Fat Free Beef Broth
1 (8-ounce) can Hunt's Tomato Sauce
1 (15-ounce) can diced tomatoes, undrained
⅛ teaspoon black pepper
2 cups uncooked macaroni
1 (2.5-ounce) jar sliced mushrooms, drained

In a large skillet sprayed with butter-flavored cooking spray, brown meat and onion. Stir in beef broth, tomato sauce, undrained tomatoes, and black pepper. Bring mixture to a boil. Add uncooked macaroni and mushrooms. Mix well to combine. Lower heat, cover, and simmer for 15 to 20 minutes or until macaroni is tender, stirring occasionally.

Each serving equals:

HE: 2 Meat • 1½ Vegetable • 1 Bread •
8 Optional Calories

229 Calories • 5 gm Fat • 20 gm Protein •
26 gm Carbohydrate • 549 mg Sodium •
26 mg Calcium • 3 gm Fiber

DIABETIC EXCHANGES: 2 Meat • 1½ Starch •
1 Vegetable

Majestic Cheesecake Tarts

● Serves 6

1 (8-ounce) package Philadelphia fat-free cream cheese
1 (4-serving) package JELL-O sugar-free instant chocolate
    pudding mix
⅔ cup Carnation Nonfat Dry Milk Powder
1 cup water
¼ cup Cool Whip Free
½ teaspoon coconut extract
½ teaspoon almond extract
1 (6-single serve) package Keebler graham cracker crusts
1 tablespoon slivered almonds
1 tablespoon mini chocolate chips
1 tablespoon flaked coconut

In a large bowl, stir cream cheese with a sturdy spoon until
soft. Add dry pudding mix, dry milk powder, and water. Mix well
using a wire whisk. Blend in Cool Whip Free, coconut extract, and
almond extract. Evenly spoon mixture into graham cracker crusts.
In a small bowl, combine almonds, chocolate chips, and coconut.
Sprinkle about 1½ teaspoons mixture over top of each tart. Refrigerate for at least 30 minutes.

Each serving equals:

HE: 1 Bread • ⅔ Protein • ⅓ Fat Free Milk • ¼ Fat •
¼ Slider • 16 Optional Calories

227 Calories • 7 gm Fat • 11 gm Protein •
30 gm Carbohydrate • 502 mg Sodium •
210 mg Calcium • 1 gm Fiber

DIABETIC EXCHANGES: 1 Starch • 1 Fat •
1 Other Carbohydrate • ½ Meat

Sparkling Orange Spritzer

○ Serves 6 (¾ cup)

1½ cups cold unsweetened orange juice
1½ cups cold Diet Mountain Dew
2 cups ice cubes

In a blender container, combine orange juice and Diet Mountain Dew. Add ice cubes. Cover and process on BLEND for 15 to 20 seconds or until mixture is thick and smooth. Serve at once.

Each serving equals:

HE: ½ Fruit

---

24 Calories • 0 gm Fat • 0 gm Protein •
6 gm Carbohydrate • 7 mg Sodium • 5 mg Calcium •
0 gm Fiber

DIABETIC EXCHANGES: ½ Fruit

Luscious Russian Repast

There's no borscht on the menu here, but since it features an entrée inspired by a favorite Russian dish, the creamy stroganoff beloved by tsars and peasants alike, I thought that calling it luscious was fair—and it's just Russian enough!

THE PLAN: I've always been known as "the Pie Lady," and the dessert for this meal is one of the reasons why. **Rocky Road Peanut Butter Pie** is as outrageously good as it sounds, and contains so many "treat" ingredients, it's almost too good to be true—but it is. Once you've placed it in the refrigerator, why not start the **Chilled Fruit Salad,** which gets better and better as it gets cold. The sweet carrots add lots of crunch. Now for the **Hamburger Stroganoff,** a creamy, saucy blend that turns basic into brilliant. Serve it with **Pimiento Green Beans,** and you'll feel warm enough inside to survive a journey to Siberia!

Chilled Fruit Salad

❂ Serves 6 (½ cup)

1½ cups (3 small) cored, unpeeled, and chopped
     Red Delicious apples
1 (8-ounce) can pineapple tidbits, packed in fruit juice,
     drained and ¼ cup liquid reserved
1 (11-ounce) can mandarin oranges, rinsed and drained
1 cup shredded carrots
2 tablespoons Splenda Granular

In a medium bowl, combine apples, pineapple tidbits, mandarin oranges, and carrots. In a small bowl, combine reserved pineapple liquid and Splenda. Add liquid mixture to fruit mixture. Mix well to coat. Cover and refrigerate for at least 15 minutes. Gently stir again just before serving.

Each serving equals:

HE: 1 Fruit • ⅓ Vegetable • 12 Optional Calories

64 Calories • 0 gm Fat • 0 gm Protein •
16 gm Carbohydrate • 8 mg Sodium •
16 mg Calcium • 2 gm Fiber

DIABETIC EXCHANGES: 1 Fruit

Pimiento Green Beans

O Serves 6 (scant ½ cup)

2 (15-ounce) cans cut green beans, rinsed and drained
¼ cup Kraft Fat Free Italian Dressing
1 (2-ounce) jar chopped pimiento, undrained

In a large skillet sprayed with butter-flavored cooking spray, combine green beans, Italian dressing, and undrained pimiento. Cook over medium heat for 5 to 6 minutes, or until mixture is heated through, stirring often.

Each serving equals:

HE: 1 Vegetable • 5 Optional Calories

28 Calories • 0 gm Fat • 1 gm Protein •
6 gm Carbohydrate • 406 mg Sodium •
29 mg Calcium • 2 gm Fiber

DIABETIC EXCHANGES: 1 Vegetable

Hamburger Stroganoff

Serves 6

16 ounces extra-lean ground sirloin beef or turkey breast
2 cups sliced fresh mushrooms
1 cup chopped onion
1 (12-ounce) jar Heinz Fat Free Beef Gravy
2 tablespoons reduced-sodium ketchup
1 teaspoon prepared yellow mustard
2 teaspoons dried parsley flakes
½ cup Land O Lakes no-fat sour cream
3 cups hot cooked noodles, rinsed and drained

In a large skillet sprayed with butter-flavored cooking spray, brown meat, mushrooms, and onion for 8 to 10 minutes or until vegetables are tender. Stir in beef gravy, ketchup, mustard, and parsley flakes. Lower heat and simmer for 5 minutes, stirring often. Add sour cream. Mix well to combine. Continue simmering for 2 to 3 minutes or until mixture is heated through, stirring often. For each serving, place ½ cup noodles on a plate and spoon about ¾ cup meat sauce over top.

HINT: Usually 2⅔ cups uncooked noodles cooks to about 3 cups.

Each serving equals:

HE: 2 Protein • 1 Bread • 1 Vegetable • ¼ Slider •
19 Optional Calories

249 Calories • 5 gm Fat • 21 gm Protein •
30 gm Carbohydrate • 388 mg Sodium •
45 mg Calcium • 2 gm Fiber

DIABETIC EXCHANGES: 2 Meat • 1½ Starch •
1 Vegetable

Rocky Road Peanut Butter Pie

● Serves 8

1 (4-serving) package JELL-O sugar-free instant vanilla
  pudding mix
⅔ cup Carnation Nonfat Dry Milk Powder
1¼ cups water
¼ cup Peter Pan or Skippy reduced-fat peanut butter
½ cup miniature marshmallows
2 tablespoons mini chocolate chips
1 (6-ounce) Keebler chocolate pie crust
2 tablespoons chopped dry-roasted peanuts
½ cup Cool Whip Lite

In a large bowl, combine dry pudding mix, dry milk powder, and water. Mix well using a wire whisk. Blend in peanut butter. Add marshmallows and chocolate chips. Mix gently to combine. Spread mixture evenly into pie crust. Evenly sprinkle peanuts over top. Refrigerate for at least 30 minutes. Cut into 8 servings. When serving, top each with 1 tablespoon Cool Whip Lite.

Each serving equals:

HE: 1 Bread • 1 Fat • ½ Protein • ¼ Fat Free Milk •
¼ Slider • 12 Optional Calories

222 Calories • 10 gm Fat • 5 gm Protein •
28 gm Carbohydrate • 346 mg Sodium •
76 mg Calcium • 1 gm Fiber

DIABETIC EXCHANGES: 1 Starch •
1 Other Carbohydrate • 1 Fat

Try These Tacos!

I've discovered that lots of my readers go out for Mexican food but rarely if ever try to prepare it at home. Is it because the ingredients seem too exotic, or that they don't have the right recipes? Or do they fear it's just too time-consuming? Whatever the possible reasons may be, I'm here to change all that with a fast, fun, and festive menu that features South of the Border–style favorites.

THE PLAN: Let's start with some lively colors in my **Grande Corn Relish**, which takes just seconds to mix, and will intensify in flavor in the refrigerator. Now you're ready to make the **Gringo Tacos**, a perfect introduction to this beloved classic. You may want to set up your "fixin's" in advance, because once the meat is ready, the meal is ready. **Hacienda "Refried" Beans** taste like the real thing but without all that unhealthy fat. Just "heat-'em-and-eat-'em"! Dessert should be heated right before serving, and oh, won't your family just love my **Hot Apple Pie Sundaes.** Find a radio station with a spicy beat, and you're ready to spend an evening in Mexico!

Grande Corn Relish

○ Serves 4 (½ cup)

¼ cup finely chopped onion
¼ cup finely chopped green bell pepper
½ cup chunky salsa (mild, medium, or hot)
½ teaspoon dried minced garlic
1 tablespoon Splenda Granular
⅛ teaspoon black pepper
1 tablespoon chopped fresh parsley or cilantro
1 (15-ounce) can whole-kernel corn, rinsed and drained

In a medium bowl, combine onion, green pepper, and salsa. Stir in garlic, Splenda, black pepper, and parsley. Add corn. Mix well to combine. Cover and refrigerate for at least 30 minutes. Gently stir again just before serving.

Each serving equals:

HE: 1 Bread • ½ Vegetable • 1 Optional Calorie

116 Calories • 0 gm Fat • 4 gm Protein •
25 gm Carbohydrate • 476 mg Sodium •
10 mg Calcium • 3 gm Fiber

DIABETIC EXCHANGES: 1 Starch • ½ Vegetable

Hacienda "Refried" Beans

◑ Serves 4 (Scant ½ cup)

1 (15-ounce) can pinto beans, rinsed and drained
½ cup chunky salsa (mild, medium, or hot)
2 tablespoons reduced-sodium ketchup
1 tablespoon water
1 teaspoon chili seasoning
1 teaspoon dried parsley flakes

In a medium bowl, mash pinto beans with a potato masher or fork. Stir in salsa, ketchup, water, chili seasoning, and parsley flakes. Spread mixture into a large skillet sprayed with butter-flavored cooking spray. Cook over medium heat for 6 to 8 minutes or until mixture is heated through, stirring often.

Each serving equals:

HE: ¾ Protein • ½ Bread • ¼ Vegetable •
8 Optional Calories

---

89 Calories • 1 gm Fat • 4 gm Protein •
16 gm Carbohydrate • 336 mg Sodium •
34 mg Calcium • 4 gm Fiber

DIABETIC EXCHANGES: 1 Starch • ½ Meat

Gringo Tacos

○ Serves 4

8 ounces extra-lean ground sirloin beef or turkey breast
½ cup chopped onion
1 cup taco sauce
4 cups finely shredded lettuce
3 cups WOW! Nacho chips or baked tortilla chips,
   broken into large pieces
¾ cup shredded Kraft reduced-fat Cheddar cheese
¼ cup Land O Lakes no-fat sour cream

In a large skillet sprayed with butter-flavored cooking spray, brown meat and onion. Stir in taco sauce. For each serving, place 1 cup lettuce on a plate, arrange ¾ cup chips over lettuce, spoon a scant ½ cup meat sauce over chips, sprinkle 3 tablespoons Cheddar cheese over meat sauce, and top with 1 tablespoon sour cream.

Each serving equals:

HE: 2½ Protein • 1¾ Vegetable • 1 Bread •
15 Optional Calories

255 Calories • 7 gm Fat • 20 gm Protein •
28 gm Carbohydrate • 679 mg Sodium •
223 mg Calcium • 2 gm Fiber

DIABETIC EXCHANGES: 2½ Meat • 1½ Vegetable •
1 Other Carbohydrate

Hot Apple Pie Sundaes

○ Serves 4

1 (20-ounce) can Lucky Leaf No Sugar Added Apple Pie Filling
¼ cup Splenda Granular
1½ teaspoons apple pie spice
2 cups Wells' Blue Bunny sugar- and fat-free vanilla ice cream
  or any sugar- and fat-free ice cream

In a medium saucepan, combine apple pie filling, Splenda, and apple pie spice. Cook over medium heat for 5 to 6 minutes or until mixture is hot, stirring often. For each serving, place ½ cup ice cream in a dessert dish and spoon about ½ cup hot apple mixture over top. Serve at once.

Each serving equals:

HE: 1 Fruit • ½ Fat Free Milk • ½ Slider •
1 Optional Calorie

---

144 Calories • 0 gm Fat • 4 gm Protein •
32 gm Carbohydrate • 67 mg Sodium •
127 mg Calcium • 2 gm Fiber

DIABETIC EXCHANGES: 1 Fruit • 1 Other Carbohydrate

Roman Holiday

Some of you may remember the glorious film by the same name, starring Gregory Peck as the newspaper reporter and the irresistible Audrey Hepburn as a runaway princess who longs for a taste of real life. Shot in black-and-white, this classic film invites all who watch it to an unforgettable party, full of color and fun and the romance that is Rome. Even if you've never seen the Eternal City in person, why not rent the movie and enjoy it after this sumptuous Italian feast?

THE PLAN: Start with the meal's bookends, which both need a bit of chilling to reach their peak of flavor. **Chunky Cucumber and Tomato Salad** is crunchy and refreshing, and it's quickly ready for the fridge. **Layered Pistachio Parfaits** sound just as scrumptious as they look. Chill them while you make dinner, and dessert will delight every diner. Next, make the **Roman Baked Potato Strips**, which are transformed in your oven into astonishingly tasty treats. Finally, my **Italian Meat Patties** are headed for your skillet, where they brown while you prepare the luscious sauce. While they simmer, set the table and warm up the VCR. As the Italians say, *Buona sera!* (Good evening!)

Chunky Cucumber and Tomato Salad

○ Serves 6 (½ cup)

¼ cup Kraft fat-free mayonnaise
1 tablespoon white distilled vinegar
1 tablespoon Splenda Granular
¼ teaspoon Italian seasoning
2 cups chopped fresh tomatoes
1 cup diced unpeeled cucumber

In a medium bowl, combine mayonnaise, vinegar, Splenda, and Italian seasoning. Add tomatoes and cucumber. Mix gently to combine. Cover and refrigerate for at least 15 minutes. Gently stir again just before serving.

Each serving equals:

HE: 1 Vegetable, 4 Optional Calories

20 Calories • 0 gm Fat • 0 gm Protein •
5 gm Carbohydrate • 85 mg Sodium •
6 mg Calcium • 1 gm Fiber

DIABETIC EXCHANGES: 1 Vegetable

Roman Baked Potato Strips

○ Serves 6

½ cup Kraft Fat Free Italian Dressing
3 tablespoons dried fine bread crumbs
¼ cup Kraft Reduced Fat Parmesan Style Grated Topping
5 cups unpeeled raw potato strips

Preheat oven to 400 degrees. Cover a baking sheet with aluminum foil. Spray foil with olive oil–flavored cooking spray. Place Italian dressing in a shallow saucer. In a self-seal sandwich bag, combine bread crumbs and Parmesan cheese. Dip potato strips first in Italian dressing, then shake in bread crumb mixture to coat. Place coated potatoes on prepared baking sheet. Drizzle any remaining dressing and crumbs over top. Bake for 30 minutes. Divide into 6 servings.

Each serving equals:

HE: 1 Bread • ¼ Slider • 1 Optional Calorie

129 Calories • 1 gm Fat • 3 gm Protein •
27 gm Carbohydrate • 345 mg Sodium •
48 mg Calcium • 2 gm Fiber

DIABETIC EXCHANGES: 1½ Starch

Italian Meat Patties

☻ Serves 6

> 16 ounces extra-lean ground sirloin beef or turkey breast
> 6 tablespoons dried fine bread crumbs
> 2 teaspoons Italian seasoning☆
> 1 (10¾-ounce) can Healthy Request Tomato Soup
> ¾ cup shredded Kraft reduced-fat mozzarella cheese

In a large bowl, combine meat, bread crumbs, and 1 teaspoon Italian seasoning. Using a ⅓ cup measuring cup as a guide, form into 6 patties. Place patties in large skillet sprayed with olive oil–flavored cooking spray. Brown patties for 3 to 4 minutes on each side. Meanwhile, in a medium bowl, combine tomato soup and remaining 1 teaspoon Italian seasoning. Pour soup mixture evenly over browned patties. Lower heat, cover, and simmer for 10 minutes. Sprinkle 2 tablespoons mozzarella cheese over top of each patty. Recover and continue simmering for 2 minutes or until cheese starts to melt. For each serving, place a patty on a plate and evenly spoon any remaining sauce over top.

Each serving equals:

HE: 2⅔ Protein • ⅓ Bread • ¼ Slider •
10 Optional Calories

---

182 Calories • 6 gm Fat • 20 gm Protein •
12 gm Carbohydrate • 362 mg Sodium •
107 mg Calcium • 0 gm Fiber

DIABETIC EXCHANGES: 2½ Meat •
½ Other Carbohydrate

Layered Pistachio Parfaits

● Serves 6

> 1 (4-serving) package JELL-O sugar-free instant pistachio
>   pudding mix
> 1 (12-fluid-ounce) can Carnation Evaporated Fat Free Milk
> ¾ cup Cool Whip Free☆
> 9 (2½-inch) chocolate graham cracker squares, made into
>   coarse crumbs
> 2 tablespoons mini chocolate chips

In a medium bowl, combine dry pudding mix and evaporated milk. Mix well using a wire whisk. Gently blend in 6 tablespoons Cool Whip Free. Spoon about 2 tablespoons pudding mixture into 6 parfait dishes. Evenly divide graham cracker crumbs over top of each. Spoon another 2 tablespoons pudding mixture into each parfait dish. Top each with 1 tablespoon Cool Whip Free and ½ teaspoon chocolate chips. Refrigerate for at least 15 minutes.

HINT: A self-seal sandwich bag works great for crushing graham crackers.

Each serving equals:

HE: ½ Fat Free Milk • ½ Bread • ½ Slider •
4 Optional Calories

---

109 Calories • 1 gm Fat • 5 gm Protein •
20 gm Carbohydrate • 322 mg Sodium •
160 mg Calcium • 0 gm Fiber

DIABETIC EXCHANGES: ½ Fat Free Milk • ½ Starch •
½ Other Carbohydrate

Sunny Salad Days

Even if it's dreary and cold outside, you can bring a load of sunshine into your kitchen with this menu. It begins with a salad that shimmers with sunny flavors; it features a main dish that will remind you of fun summer barbecues; and it ends with a dessert so warming and comforting that you'll almost expect to wake up next morning to find that it's July!

THE PLAN: Preheat your oven to 400 degrees to get ready to make your entrée and dessert first. Both the **Barbequed Burger Cups** and the **Cinnamon Peach Cobbler** require about the same cooking and resting time. If you've got the time, make the cobbler first and let it set. (You may choose to reheat it a bit just before dessert is served—if your family likes it that way.) Then it's time to make your veggie side dish, a lovely and quick **Peas Supreme.** Throw together the ingredients of your **Sunshine Tossed Salad,** and dinner's on the table! Don't forget the sunscreen . . .

Sunshine Tossed Salad

○ Serves 4 (1 cup)

2 tablespoons Kraft fat-free mayonnaise
2 tablespoons orange marmalade spreadable fruit
¼ cup Kraft Fat Free Catalina Dressing
1½ teaspoons dried minced onion flakes
1½ teaspoons dried parsley flakes
1½ teaspoons Worcestershire sauce
⅛ teaspoon black pepper
4 cups finely shredded lettuce

In a large bowl, combine mayonnaise, orange marmalade spreadable fruit, and Catalina dressing. Stir in onion flakes, parsley flakes, Worcestershire, and black pepper. Add lettuce. Toss well to coat. Serve at once.

Each serving equals:

HE: 1 Vegetable • ½ Fruit • ¼ Slider •
3 Optional Calories

---

56 Calories • 0 gm Fat • 1 gm Protein •
13 gm Carbohydrate • 261 mg Sodium •
32 mg Calcium • 2 gm Fiber

DIABETIC EXCHANGES: 1 Vegetable • ½ Fruit

Peas Supreme

☻ Serves 4 (½ cup)

2 cups frozen peas, thawed
1 tablespoon + 1 teaspoon I Can't Believe It's Not Butter!
Light Margarine
1 (2.5-ounce) jar button mushrooms, drained
1 (2-ounce) jar chopped pimiento, drained
1 teaspoon dried parsley flakes
⅛ teaspoon black pepper

In a medium saucepan sprayed with butter-flavored cooking spray, combine peas and margarine. Stir in mushrooms, pimiento, parsley flakes, and black pepper. Cook over medium heat for 5 to 6 minutes or until mixture is heated through, stirring often.

HINT: Thaw peas by placing in a colander and rinsing under hot water for 1 minute.

Each serving equals:

HE: 1 Bread • ½ Fat • ¼ Vegetable

78 Calories • 2 gm Fat • 4 gm Protein •
11 gm Carbohydrate • 201 mg Sodium •
21 mg Calcium • 4 gm Fiber

DIABETIC EXCHANGES: 1 Starch • ½ Fat

Barbequed Burger Cups

● Serves 4

2 tablespoons Splenda Granular
½ cup reduced-sodium ketchup☆
½ teaspoon prepared yellow mustard
12 ounces extra-lean ground sirloin beef or turkey breast
¾ cup crushed cornflakes
1 teaspoon dried onion flakes
⅛ teaspoon black pepper

Preheat oven to 400 degrees. Spray 4 wells of a muffin pan with butter-flavored cooking spray. In a large bowl, combine Splenda, ¼ cup ketchup, and mustard. Add meat, cornflakes, onion flakes, and black pepper. Mix well to combine. Divide mixture into 4 portions. Form each portion into a ball and place in prepared muffin wells. Top each with 1 tablespoon ketchup. Bake for 30 minutes. Place muffin pan on a wire rack and let set for 5 minutes.

HINT: Fill unused muffin wells with water. It protects the muffin pan and ensures even baking.

Each serving equals:

HE: 2¼ Protein • ½ Bread • ¼ Slider • 13 Optional Calories

176 Calories • 4 gm fat • 18 gm Protein • 17 gm Carbohydrate • 174 mg Sodium • 7 mg Calcium • 1 gm Fiber

DIABETIC EXCHANGES: 2 Meat • ½ Starch • ½ Other Carbohydrate

Cinnamon Peach Cobbler

● Serves 6

3 cups (6 medium) peeled and sliced fresh peaches
1 cup Splenda Granular☆
1 tablespoon lemon juice
1 (7.5-ounce) can Pillsbury refrigerated buttermilk biscuits
1 teaspoon ground cinnamon

Preheat oven to 400 degrees. Spray an 8-by-8-inch baking dish with butter-flavored cooking spray. In a large bowl, combine peaches, ¾ cup Splenda, and lemon juice. Spoon fruit mixture into prepared baking dish. Separate biscuits and cut each into 3 pieces. Evenly sprinkle biscuit pieces over fruit mixture. In a small bowl, combine cinnamon and remaining ¼ cup Splenda. Sprinkle cinnamon mixture over top of biscuit pieces. Lightly spray top with butter-flavored cooking spray. Bake for 30 minutes. Lightly spray tops again with butter-flavored cooking spray. Place baking dish on a wire rack and let set for at least 5 minutes. Divide into 6 servings.

HINTS: 1. Frozen unsweetened sliced peaches, which have been thawed, may be substituted for fresh peaches.
2. Good served warm with a scoop of sugar- and fat-free vanilla ice cream, but don't forget to count the calories accordingly.

Each serving equals:

HE: 1¼ Bread • 1 Fruit • 16 Optional Calories

141 Calories • 1 gm Fat • 3 gm Protein •
30 gm Carbohydrate • 303 mg Sodium •
8 mg Calcium • 2 gm Fiber

DIABETIC EXCHANGES: 1 Starch • 1 Fruit

Pasta and Chocolate

This menu is made up of cozy comfort foods to please kids of any age, featuring two of nearly every family's Top Ten. I bet it will quickly become your "go-to" plan when you haven't got a lot of time but want to satisfy those ravenous appetites seated around your kitchen table. And why not? It's easy and it's oh-so-good!

THE PLAN: **Chocolate Upside Down Pudding Cake** sounds out of this world, doesn't it? It might just be the best quick cake I've developed in years, and it's the best place to start on this menu. Once dessert is in the oven, you can brown your meat for **Cheeseburger Pasta** and add the rotini. While your entrée simmers, make **Italian Green Beans** and **Lazy Lettuce and Tomato Salad.** Quick, quick, quick, from stovetop to tabletop, which means more time to eat and enjoy.

Lazy Lettuce and Tomato Salad

○ Serves 4

4 cups finely shredded lettuce
1 cup chopped fresh tomato
⅓ cup Kraft Fat Free Thousand Island Dressing
2 tablespoons Land O Lakes no-fat sour cream
1 teaspoon dried parsley flakes

Evenly arrange 1 cup lettuce on 4 salad plates. Top each with ¼ cup tomatoes. In a small bowl, combine Thousand Island dressing, sour cream, and parsley flakes. Drizzle about 2 tablespoons dressing mixture over top of each salad. Serve at once.

Each serving equals:

HE: 1½ Vegetable • ¼ Slider • 14 Optional Calories

52 Calories • 0 gm Fat • 1 gm Protein •
12 gm Carbohydrate • 169 mg Sodium •
39 mg Calcium • 2 gm Fiber

DIABETIC EXCHANGES: 1½ Vegetable

Italian Green Beans

○ Serves 4 (¾ cup)

½ cup chopped onion
1 (15-ounce) can cut green beans, rinsed and drained
¼ cup Oscar Mayer or Hormel Real Bacon Bits
⅓ cup Kraft Fat Free Italian Dressing
1 (2-ounce) jar chopped pimiento, drained

In a medium saucepan sprayed with butter-flavored cooking spray, sauté onion for 5 minutes. Stir in green beans and bacon bits. Add Italian dressing and pimiento. Mix well to combine. Continue cooking for 5 minutes or until mixture is heated through, stirring occasionally.

Each serving equals:

HE: 1¼ Vegetable • ¼ Slider • 16 Optional Calories

86 Calories • 2 gm Fat • 5 gm Protein •
12 gm Carbohydrate • 440 mg Sodium •
56 mg Calcium • 3 gm Fiber

DIABETIC EXCHANGES: 1½ Vegetable • ½ Meat

Cheeseburger Pasta

○ Serves 4 (scant 1 cup)

8 ounces extra-lean ground sirloin beef or turkey breast
1 (10¾-ounce) can Healthy Request Tomato Soup
1¼ cups water
1 cup cubed Velveeta Light processed cheese
1 cup uncooked rotini pasta

In a large skillet sprayed with butter-flavored cooking spray, brown meat. Stir in tomato soup, water, and Velveeta cheese. Add uncooked rotini pasta. Mix well to combine. Lower heat, cover, and simmer for 10 to 15 minutes or until pasta is tender, stirring occasionally.

Each serving equals:

HE: 2½ Protein • ¾ Bread • ½ Slider •
5 Optional Calories

267 Calories • 7 gm Fat • 20 gm Protein •
31 gm Carbohydrate • 605 mg Sodium •
167 mg Calcium • 1 gm Fiber

DIABETIC EXCHANGES: 2½ Meat • 1 Starch •
½ Other Carbohydrate

Chocolate Upside Down Pudding Cake

○ Serves 8

2 cups Splenda Granular☆
3 tablespoons unsweetened
　cocoa powder☆
1 cup all-purpose flour
1½ teaspoons baking powder
¼ teaspoon table salt

½ cup fat-free milk
2 tablespoons vegetable oil
1½ teaspoons vanilla extract
¼ cup chopped walnuts
1 cup boiling water

Preheat oven to 350 degrees. Spray a 9-inch round cake pan with butter-flavored cooking spray. In a large bowl, combine ¾ cup Splenda, 2 tablespoons cocoa, flour, baking powder, and salt. In a small bowl, combine milk, oil, and vanilla extract. Add milk mixture to flour mixture. Mix gently just to combine. Fold in walnuts. Evenly spread batter into prepared pan. In a medium bowl, combine remaining 1¼ cups Splenda, 1 tablespoon cocoa, and boiling water. Carefully pour boiling water mixture evenly over top. Bake for 35 minutes. Place pan on a wire rack and let set for at least 10 minutes. Cut into 8 wedges.

HINTS: 1. Batter is thick but spreads easily with a spatula.
2. Good served warm with 1 scoop sugar- and fat-free vanilla or chocolate ice cream. If using, don't forget to count the additional calories.

Each serving equals:

HE: 1 Fat • ⅔ Bread • ½ Slider • 3 Optional Calories

146 Calories • 6 gm Fat • 3 gm Protein •
20 gm Carbohydrate • 142 mg Sodium •
78 mg Calcium • 1 gm Fiber

DIABETIC EXCHANGES: 1 Fat • 1 Starch

Asian Fantasy

Here's a speedy but delightfully exotic option for a night when you want to put supper on the table in just about 30 minutes—and when your mouth is watering for a taste of the Far East.

THE PLAN: They say "Life is uncertain, eat dessert first." Well, I like my meal served in the usual order, but for this menu, you begin with dessert preparation. My **Lemon Cloud Dessert** is frothy and light but also rich and rewarding. Let it rest in the refrigerator, while you get going on the other courses. Now it's on to a savory entrée, **Ground Beef Chow Mein**. Don't you just love a recipe that says, pour all these ingredients into your skillet and simmer? (Well, first you have to brown the meat, but after that, it's "everyone into the pool"!) Stir up **Oriental Iced Tea** next and chill before serving. Finally, prepare the **Mandarin Tossed Salad**, which adds a tasty citrus touch to the meal along with some bright color. Enjoy!

Mandarin Tossed Salad

◷ Serves 4 (1 cup)

4 cups shredded lettuce
1 (11-ounce) can mandarin oranges, rinsed and drained
¼ cup Kraft Fat Free French Dressing
2 tablespoons apple cider vinegar
¼ cup slivered almonds

In a large bowl, combine lettuce and mandarin oranges. In a small bowl, combine French dressing, vinegar, and almonds. Add dressing mixture to lettuce mixture. Toss gently to coat. Serve at once.

Each serving equals:

HE: 1 Vegetable • ½ Fruit • ½ Fat • ¼ Protein • ¼ Slider • 2 Optional Calories

116 Calories • 4 gm Fat • 2 gm Protein •
18 gm Carbohydrate • 162 mg Sodium •
56 mg Calcium • 2 gm Fiber

DIABETIC EXCHANGES: 1 Vegetable • 1 Fat • ½ Fruit

Ground Beef Chow Mein

🌙 Serves 4

8 ounces extra-lean ground sirloin beef or turkey breast
1 (2.5-ounce) jar sliced mushrooms, drained
2 tablespoons reduced-sodium soy sauce
½ teaspoon ground ginger
1 (12-ounce) jar Heinz Fat Free Beef Gravy
1 cup sliced celery
½ cup chopped onion
1 (14-ounce) can La Choy Chop Suey Vegetables,
*   rinsed and drained*
2 cups hot cooked rice
½ cup chow mein noodles

In a large skillet sprayed with butter-flavored cooking spray, brown meat. Stir in mushrooms, soy sauce, ginger, and beef gravy. Add celery, onion, and chop suey vegetables. Mix well to combine. Lower heat, cover, and simmer for 15 minutes, stirring occasionally. For each serving, place ½ cup rice on a plate, spoon about 1 cup meat mixture over rice, and sprinkle 2 tablespoons chow mein noodles over top.

HINT: Usually 1⅓ cups uncooked instant rice cooks to about 2 cups.

Each serving equals:

HE: 2 Vegetable • 1½ Protein • 1¼ Bread •
¼ Slider • 10 Optional Calories

217 Calories • 5 gm Fat • 16 gm Protein •
27 gm Carbohydrate • 781 mg Sodium •
44 mg Calcium • 3 gm Fiber

DIABETIC EXCHANGES: 2 Starch • 1½ Vegetable •
1½ Meat

Lemon Cloud Dessert

○ Serves 4

> 1 (4-serving) package JELL-O sugar-free vanilla
>   cook-and-serve pudding mix
> 1 (4-serving) package JELL-O sugar-free lemon gelatin
> ⅔ cup Carnation Nonfat Dry Milk Powder
> 2 cups water
> ½ cup Philadelphia fat-free cream cheese
> ¼ cup Cool Whip Lite

In a medium saucepan, combine dry pudding mix, dry gelatin, dry milk powder, and water. Mix well using a wire whisk. Cook over medium heat until mixture thickens and starts to boil, stirring constantly using a wire whisk. Remove from heat. Add cream cheese. Mix well using a wire whisk. Evenly spoon mixture into 4 parfait or dessert dishes. Refrigerate for at least 30 minutes. When serving, top each with 1 tablespoon Cool Whip Lite.

Each serving equals:

HE: ½ Fat Free Milk • ½ Protein • ¼ Slider •
15 Optional Calories

88 Calories • 0 gm Fat • 8 gm Protein •
14 gm Carbohydrate • 302 mg Sodium •
230 mg Calcium • 0 gm Fiber

DIABETIC EXCHANGES: ½ Fat Free Milk • ½ Meat •
½ Optional Calories

Oriental Iced Tea

● Serves 4

> 2 tablespoons Lipton unsweetened instant tea powder
> 3½ cups cold water
> ½ cup cold unsweetened orange juice
> 2 cups ice cubes
> 4 orange slices (optional)

In a pitcher, combine instant tea powder, cold water, and orange juice. Refrigerate for at least 15 minutes. When serving, place ½ cup ice cubes in a tall glass, pour 1 cup iced tea mixture over ice, and garnish glass with an orange slice.

Each serving equals:

HE: ¼ Fruit

---

16 Calories • 0 gm Fat • 0 gm Protein •
4 gm Carbohydrate • 2 mg Sodium •
3 mg Calcium • 0 gm Fiber

DIABETIC EXCHANGES: Free Food

California Dreaming

Remember that old Mamas and the Papas song about dreaming of California while the leaves are falling and the sky is gray? (I may be showing my age, but the song lives on!) Sometimes it just takes a delicious bite or two to transport us in spirit to a place that is warm and where the living is easy (or at least seems to be!). These dishes are perfect for a chilly fall evening when the piles of leaves are taller than your kids and you feel the first breath of winter bearing down.

THE PLAN: Even if you've got a big oven, I'd suggest making dessert first tonight, as the **Baked Raisin Custards** will just get richer and creamier as they rest. (All three bake at 350 degrees, however.) Then you're ready to slip two splendidly savory dishes into the oven—first, **Parmesan Potato Bake**, which needs just under an hour, and **Weeknight Meat Loaf**, which may need just a bit longer. When you've got just about 20 minutes to go until dinner, head for California in your heart, while fixing **California Veggies with Country Mustard Sauce.** Rain or shine, cloudy or sunny, you'll feel the warmth inside!

California Veggies with Country Mustard Sauce

◑ Serves 6 (½ cup)

4½ cups frozen broccoli, cauliflower, and carrot blend, thawed
1 cup hot water
¾ cup Land O Lakes no-fat sour cream
¼ cup fat-free milk
2 tablespoons Grey Poupon Country Style Dijon Mustard
2 teaspoons dried onion flakes
1 teaspoon dried parsley flakes

In a medium saucepan, combine vegetables and water. Cook over medium heat for 6 to 8 minutes or just until vegetables are tender. Drain and return vegetables to saucepan. In a small bowl, combine sour cream, milk, mustard, onion flakes, and parsley flakes. Stir sour cream mixture into vegetable mixture. Lower heat and simmer for 6 to 8 minutes or until mixture is heated through, stirring occasionally.

HINT: Thaw vegetables by placing in a colander and rinsing under hot water for 1 minute.

Each serving equals:

HE: 1½ Vegetable • ¼ Slider • 14 Optional Calories

56 Calories • 0 gm Fat • 4 gm Protein •
10 gm Carbohydrate • 186 mg Sodium •
75 mg Calcium • 2 gm Fiber

DIABETIC EXCHANGES: 1½ Vegetable •
½ Other Carbohydrate

Parmesan Potato Bake

● Serves 6

6 cups shredded loose-packed frozen potatoes
1 (10¾-ounce) can Healthy Request Cream of Mushroom
      Soup
⅓ cup Land O Lakes Fat Free Half & Half
1 tablespoon dried onion flakes
2 teaspoons dried parsley flakes
6 tablespoons Kraft Reduced Fat Parmesan Style
      Grated Topping

Preheat oven to 350 degrees. Spray an 8-by-12-inch baking dish with butter-flavored cooking spray. In a large bowl, combine potatoes, mushroom soup, half & half, onion flakes, and parsley flakes. Evenly spread mixture into prepared baking dish. Sprinkle Parmesan cheese evenly over top. Lightly spray top with butter-flavored cooking spray. Bake for 45 to 50 minutes. Place baking dish on a wire rack and let set for 5 minutes. Divide into 6 servings.

HINT: Mr. Dell's frozen shredded potatoes are a good choice or raw shredded potatoes, rinsed and patted dry, may be used in place of frozen potatoes.

Each serving equals:

HE: ⅔ Bread • ¼ Protein • ¼ Slider •
17 Optional Calories

121 Calories • 1 gm Fat • 4 gm Protein •
24 gm Carbohydrate • 210 mg Sodium •
75 mg Calcium • 3 gm Fiber

DIABETIC EXCHANGES: 1 Starch •
½ Other Carbohydrate

Weeknight Meat Loaf

🌙 Serves 6

16 ounces extra-lean ground sirloin beef or turkey breast
15 small fat-free saltine crackers, made into crumbs
1 cup finely chopped onion
1 (8-ounce) can Hunt's Tomato Sauce☆
1 (2-ounce) jar chopped pimiento, drained
1 tablespoon Splenda Granular
1 teaspoon dried parsley flakes
2 tablespoons chili sauce

Preheat oven to 350 degrees. Spray a 9-by-5-inch loaf pan with butter-flavored cooking spray. In a large bowl, combine meat, cracker crumbs, onion, ¼ cup tomato sauce, pimiento, Splenda, and parsley flakes. Mix well to combine. Pat mixture into prepared loaf pan. In a small bowl, combine remaining ¾ cup tomato sauce and chili sauce. Drizzle sauce mixture evenly over top of meat loaf. Bake for 55 to 60 minutes. Place loaf pan on a wire rack and let set for 5 minutes. Divide into 6 servings.

HINT: A self-seal sandwich bag works great for crushing crackers.

Each serving equals:

HE: 2 Protein • 1 Vegetable • ½ Bread •
7 Optional Calories

177 Calories • 5 gm Fat • 17 gm Protein •
16 gm Carbohydrate • 389 mg Sodium •
15 mg Calcium • 2 gm Fiber

DIABETIC EXCHANGES: 2 Meat • 1 Vegetable • ½ Starch

Baked Raisin Custards

● Serve 6

> 2 (4-serving) packages JELL-O sugar-free vanilla
>   cook-and-serve pudding mix
> 1 cup Carnation Nonfat Dry Milk Powder
> 3 cups water
> ¼ cup Splenda Granular☆
> ¾ cup seedless raisins
> 1 teaspoon vanilla extract
> ½ teaspoon ground cinnamon

Preheat oven to 350 degrees. Spray 6 (8-ounce) custard cups with butter-flavored cooking spray. In a medium saucepan, combine dry pudding mixes, dry milk powder, and water. Stir in 2 tablespoons Splenda and raisins. Cook over medium heat until mixture thickens and starts to boil, stirring constantly. Remove from heat. Stir in vanilla extract. Evenly spoon hot mixture into prepared custard cups. In a small bowl, combine cinnamon and remaining 2 tablespoons Splenda. Evenly sprinkle about 1 teaspoon cinnamon mixture over top of each. Place custard cups on a baking sheet. Bake for 30 minutes. Place custard cups on a wire rack and let set for at least 5 minutes.

HINT: Good warm or cold.

Each serving equals:

HE: 1 Fruit • ½ Fat Free Milk • ¼ Slider •
11 Optional Calories

---

128 Calories • 0 gm Fat • 4 gm Protein •
28 gm Carbohydrate • 208 mg Sodium •
163 mg Calcium • 1 gm Fiber

DIABETIC EXCHANGES: 1 Fruit • ½ Fat Free Milk

Beef 'N' Biscuits

This is a true all-American menu, with an apple pie for dessert and a hearty beef stew to warm you inside and out! And even if your mom or grandma never made her own biscuits, you're about to learn how. It couldn't be easier, really, and these are particularly rich and cheesy. There's something about biscuits that just say "Welcome home, I've missed you, how was your day?" Isn't it great that you can serve homemade bread in less than 15 minutes?

THE PLAN: I'm not sure who "Betty" was or why she had a beloved classic dessert named for her, but she definitely knew her apples! **Apple Betty Pie** needs 45 minutes in the oven and about 30 more to rest, so make sure you have enough time to get it ready. Most people think it should take hours, but in fact my **Stove Top Beef Stew** is done in under an hour—yum, yum! Mix up **Crisp Cabbage Slaw** and give it 30 minutes in the fridge to blend its flavors. With about 15 minutes until dinner, you make the **Cheesy Drop Biscuits**. They're so good, you might have to make a double batch!

Crisp Cabbage Slaw

○ Serves 4 (¾ cup)

½ cup Kraft fat-free mayonnaise
2 tablespoons white distilled vinegar
2 tablespoons Splenda Granular
1 teaspoon prepared yellow mustard
1 teaspoon dried parsley flakes
2 cups purchased coleslaw mix
½ cup diced unpeeled cucumber
½ cup chopped celery

In a medium bowl, combine mayonnaise, vinegar, Splenda, mustard, and parsley flakes. Add coleslaw mix, cucumber, and celery. Mix well to combine. Cover and refrigerate for at least 30 minutes. Gently stir again just before serving.

HINT: 1½ cups shredded cabbage and ½ cup shredded carrots may be used in place of purchased coleslaw mix.

Each serving equals:

HE: 1 Vegetable • ¼ Slider • 3 Optional Calories

45 Calories • 1 gm Fat • 1 gm Protein •
8 gm Carbohydrate • 258 mg Sodium •
31 mg Calcium • 2 gm Fiber

DIABETIC EXCHANGES: 1 Vegetable

Stove Top Beef Stew

● Serves 4 (1¼ cups)

3 tablespoons all-purpose flour
1 teaspoon dried parsley flakes
⅛ teaspoon black pepper
16 ounces lean sirloin steak, cut into 24 pieces
1 (12-ounce) jar Heinz Fat Free Savory Beef Gravy
1 teaspoon Worcestershire sauce
1 cup chopped onion
1½ cups chopped carrots
2 cups diced raw potatoes

In a shallow saucer, combine flour, parsley flakes, and black pepper. Evenly coat steak pieces with flour mixture. Place coated steak pieces in a large saucepan sprayed with butter-flavored cooking spray. Brown for 2 to 3 minutes on each side. Stir in beef gravy, Worcestershire, and any remaining flour mixture. Add onion, carrots, and potatoes. Mix well to combine. Lower heat, cover, and simmer for 30 to 40 minutes or until meat and vegetables are tender, stirring occasionally.

Each serving equals:

HE: 3 Protein • 1¼ Vegetable • ¾ Bread • ¼ Slider • 2 Optional Calories

272 Calories • 4 gm Fat • 30 gm Protein • 29 gm Carbohydrate • 551 mg Sodium • 34 mg Calcium • 3 gm Fiber

DIABETIC EXCHANGES: 3 Meat • 1½ Starch • 1 Vegetable

Cheesy Drop Biscuits

● Serves 4

¾ cup Bisquick Reduced Fat Baking Mix
6 tablespoons shredded Kraft reduced-fat Cheddar cheese
1 teaspoon dried onion flakes
1 teaspoon dried parsley flakes
1 tablespoon Land O Lakes no-fat sour cream
¼ cup fat-free milk

Preheat oven to 375 degrees. Spray a baking sheet with butter-flavored cooking spray. In a medium bowl, combine baking mix, Cheddar cheese, onion flakes, and parsley flakes. Add sour cream and milk. Mix well to combine. Drop by tablespoonful onto prepared baking sheet to form 4 biscuits. Bake for 8 to 10 minutes or until golden brown. Place baking sheet on a wire rack and let set for 2 to 3 minutes. Serve warm.

Each serving equals:

HE: 1 Bread • ½ Protein • 9 Optional Calories

124 Calories • 4 gm Fat • 5 gm Protein •
17 gm Carbohydrate • 244 mg Sodium •
123 mg Calcium • 1 gm Fiber

DIABETIC EXCHANGES: 1 Starch • ½ Meat

Apple Betty Pie

☻ Serves 8

1 (20-ounce) can Lucky Leaf No Sugar Added Apple Pie Filling
¼ cup unsweetened orange juice
¾ cup purchased graham cracker crumbs or 6 (2½-inch) graham
    cracker squares, made into crumbs☆
½ cup Splenda Granular☆
1 (6-ounce) Keebler graham cracker pie crust
1½ teaspoons apple pie spice
1 tablespoon + 1 teaspoon I Can't Believe It's Not Butter!
    Light Margarine

Preheat oven to 375 degrees. In a medium bowl, combine apple pie filling, orange juice, 2 tablespoons graham cracker crumbs, and ¼ cup Splenda. Spoon mixture into pie crust. In a small bowl, combine remaining 10 tablespoons graham cracker crumbs, remaining ¼ cup Splenda, apple pie spice, and margarine. Mix with a pastry blender or fork until mixture is crumbly. Evenly sprinkle crumb mixture over filling. Bake for 45 minutes. Place pie plate on a wire rack and let set for at least 30 minutes. Cut into 8 servings. Good warm or cold.

HINT: A self-seal sandwich bag works great for crushing graham crackers.

Each serving equals:

HE: 1½ Bread • ½ Fruit • ½ Fat • 10 Optional Calories

183 Calories • 7 gm Fat • 2 gm Protein •
28 gm Carbohydrate • 203 mg Sodium •
7 mg Calcium • 2 gm Fiber

DIABETIC EXCHANGES: 1½ Starch • 1 Fat • ½ Fruit

A Kitchen Barbecue

For those who live in chillier climates, the barbecue season is never long enough. For others, well, sometimes it just seems like too much work to set up and clean the outdoor grill, and so we reserve it for special occasions. Tonight, you'll enjoy that outdoor barbecue taste from your oven, with easy cleanup and flavor that's smoky and savory all at once. And hurray, you've got chocolate for dessert!

THE PLAN: For all you brownie-lovers out there, my **Brownie Puddings** are almost too good to be true! I'd get them ready first, before dedicating the oven to a sumptuous potato dish (**French Baked Potato Slices**) and the evening's main attraction, **Oven Barbequed Swiss Steak.** Both need just under an hour. Start by browning the steaks and preparing the potatoes (separately, of course), and then slip both dishes into the oven. While they bake, make the **Calico Slaw** and let it get nice and cold. Winter, spring, summer, or fall—this menu is a four-season spectacular!

Calico Slaw

● Serves 4 (¾ cup)

1½ cups finely shredded red cabbage
1½ cups finely shredded green cabbage
1 cup finely shredded carrots
½ cup Kraft fat-free mayonnaise
1 tablespoon white distilled vinegar
1 tablespoon Splenda Granular
⅛ teaspoon black pepper

In a medium bowl, combine red cabbage, green cabbage, and carrots. In a small bowl, combine mayonnaise, vinegar, Splenda, and black pepper. Add mayonnaise mixture to cabbage mixture. Mix well to combine. Cover and refrigerate for at least 15 minutes. Gently stir again just before serving.

Each serving equals:

HE: 1¼ Vegetable • ¼ Slider • 2 Optional Calories

44 Calories • 0 gm Fat • 1 gm Protein •
10 gm Carbohydrate • 237 mg Sodium •
35 mg Calcium • 2 gm Fiber

DIABETIC EXCHANGES: 1 Vegetable

French Baked Potato Slices

○ Serves 4

3 cups thinly sliced raw potatoes, rinsed and drained
¼ cup Kraft Fat Free French Dressing
2 teaspoons dried parsley flakes
1 teaspoon dried onion flakes
⅛ teaspoon black pepper

Preheat oven to 350 degrees. Spray an 8-by-8-inch baking dish with butter-flavored cooking spray. Evenly arrange potato slices in prepared baking dish. Lightly spray tops with butter-flavored cooking spray. In a small bowl, combine French dressing, parsley flakes, onion flakes, and black pepper. Drizzle dressing mixture evenly over top. Cover and bake for 30 minutes. Uncover and continue baking for 15 to 20 minutes or until potatoes are tender. Evenly divide into 4 servings. Serve at once.

Each serving equals:

HE: ¾ Bread • ¼ Slider • 3 Optional Calories

104 Calories • 0 gm Fat • 2 gm Protein •
24 gm Carbohydrate • 136 mg Sodium •
10 mg Calcium • 2 gm Fiber

DIABETIC EXCHANGES: 1½ Starch

Oven Barbequed Swiss Steak

○ Serves 4

3 tablespoons all-purpose flour

1 teaspoon dried parsley flakes

⅛ teaspoon black pepper

4 (4-ounce) lean tenderized minute or cube steaks

1 cup sliced onion

1 (8-ounce) can Hunt's Tomato Sauce

1 tablespoon Splenda Granular

1 tablespoon white distilled vinegar

1 tablespoon Worcestershire sauce

Preheat oven to 350 degrees. Spray an 8-by-8-inch baking dish with butter-flavored cooking spray. In shallow saucer, combine flour, parsley flakes, and black pepper. Evenly coat steak pieces on both sides in flour mixture. Place coated steaks in a large skillet sprayed with butter-flavored cooking spray. Brown steaks over medium heat for 3 minutes on each side. Evenly arrange meat in prepared baking dish. Sprinkle onion slices over steaks. In a small bowl, combine tomato sauce, Splenda, vinegar, Worcestershire sauce, and any remaining flour mixture. Pour sauce mixture evenly over top. Cover and bake for 45 to 55 minutes or until meat is fork-tender. When serving, evenly spoon sauce mixture over steaks.

Each serving equals:

HE: 3 Protein • 1½ Vegetable • ¼ Bread •
2 Optional Calories

192 Calories • 4 gm Fat • 27 gm Protein •
12 gm Carbohydrate • 403 mg Sodium •
27 mg Calcium • 1 gm Fiber

DIABETIC EXCHANGES: 3 Meat • 1 Vegetable

Brownie Puddings

● Serves 4

¾ cup all-purpose flour
1 cup Splenda Granular☆
¼ cup unsweetened cocoa
    powder☆
1½ teaspoons baking powder
⅔ cup fat-free milk

1 tablespoon + 1 teaspoon
    I Can't Believe It's Not
    Butter! Light Margarine
¼ cup chopped walnuts
1⅓ cups hot water

Preheat oven to 350 degrees. Spray 4 (12-ounce) custard cups with butter-flavored cooking spray. In a medium bowl, combine flour, ½ cup Splenda, 2 tablespoons cocoa, and baking powder. Add milk and margarine. Mix well just to combine. Fold in walnuts. Evenly spoon batter into prepared custard cups. In a medium bowl, combine remaining ½ cup Splenda, remaining 2 tablespoons cocoa, and hot water. Mix well using a wire whisk. Evenly pour about ⅓ cup mixture over top of each. Place custard cups on a baking sheet. Bake for 20 to 25 minutes. Place baking sheet on a wire rack and let set for 10 minutes.

HINT: Good warm or cold with Wells' Blue Bunny sugar- and fat-free vanilla ice cream or Cool Whip Lite. If using, don't forget to count the additional calories.

Each serving equals:

HE: 1 Bread • 1 Fat • ¼ Protein • ½ Slider • 11 Optional Calories

199 Calories • 7 gm Fat • 6 gm Protein • 28 gm Carbohydrate • 231 mg Sodium • 169 mg Calcium • 3 gm Fiber

DIABETIC EXCHANGES: 1 Starch • 1 Fat • ½ Other Carbohydrate

Ready for a Roast?

I've written two big cookbooks that demonstrate the many glories of your slow cooker, but most of the recipes in this book have called for the oven, the skillet, and the microwave. Now it's time to spotlight the special talents of one of my favorite kitchen appliances, what we used to call a "Crock Pot." It produces remarkably tender meat dishes and keeps all the healthy nutrients right inside the pot!

THE PLAN: This menu begins in the morning, or even the night before, when you prepare your **Crock of Roast and Veggies**. It needs 9 to 10 hours to cook, so schedule it accordingly. Everything else gets prepared closer to meal time. You can make **Anytime Peach Pie** as the name says, anytime, but I recommend at least two hours in the fridge before you top and serve it. **Sour Cream Cucumbers** are ready quickly and need to chill about 15 minutes. Finally, you'll make **Veggie Biscuits** 10 to 15 minutes before the meal, so they can be served warm.

Sour Cream Cucumbers

❂ Serves 6 (½ cup)

½ cup Land O Lakes no-fat sour cream
2 tablespoons finely minced dried chives
1 teaspoon lemon juice
2 tablespoons Splenda Granular
⅛ teaspoon black pepper
3 cups thinly sliced unpeeled cucumbers

In a large bowl, combine sour cream, chives, lemon juice, Splenda, and black pepper. Add cucumbers. Mix well to combine. Cover and refrigerate for at least 15 minutes. Gently stir again just before serving.

Each serving equals:

HE: ½ Vegetable • ¼ Slider • 2 Optional Calories

24 Calories • 0 gm Fat • 1 gm Protein •
5 gm Carbohydrate • 28 mg Sodium •
35 mg Calcium • 1 gm Fiber

DIABETIC EXCHANGES: ½ Vegetable

Crock of Roast and Veggies

● Serves 6

3 cups peeled and sliced raw potatoes, rinsed and drained
2 cups sliced carrots
1 cup chopped onion
1 (2-pound) lean beef rump roast
⅓ cup water
1 tablespoon Italian seasoning
⅛ teaspoon black pepper

Spray a slow cooker container with butter-flavored cooking spray. In prepared container, layer potatoes, carrots, and onion. Place beef roast on top of vegetables. In a small bowl, combine water, Italian seasoning, and black pepper. Pour mixture evenly over roast. Cover and cook on LOW for 9 to 10 hours. Remove roast and cut into 6 pieces. Mix vegetable mixture well. For each serving, place 1 cup vegetables on a plate, arrange meat over vegetables, and drizzle about 2 tablespoons liquid over top.

Each serving equals:

HE: 3½ Protein • 1 Vegetable • ½ Bread

243 Calories • 7 gm Fat • 26 gm Protein •
19 gm Carbohydrate • 76 mg Sodium •
26 mg Calcium • 3 gm Fiber

DIABETIC EXCHANGES: 3½ Meat • 1 Vegetable •
½ Starch

Veggie Biscuits

○ Serves 6

1 cup + 2 tablespoons Bisquick Reduced Fat Baking Mix
2 teaspoons Splenda Granular
2 tablespoons dried mixed vegetable flakes
¼ cup Land O Lakes no-fat sour cream
¼ cup Land O Lakes Fat Free Half & Half

Preheat oven to 375 degrees. Spray a baking sheet with butter-flavored cooking spray. In a medium bowl, combine baking mix, Splenda, and dried vegetable flakes. Add sour cream and half & half. Mix well just to combine. Drop batter by tablespoonful onto prepared baking sheet to form 6 biscuits. Bake for 9 minutes or until golden brown. Place baking sheet on a wire rack and let set for 2 to 3 minutes. Serve at once.

Each serving equals:

HE: 1 Bread • 17 Optional Calories

97 Calories • 1 gm Fat • 2 gm Protein • 20 gm Carbohydrate • 264 mg Sodium • 55 mg Calcium • 1 gm Fiber

DIABETIC EXCHANGES: 1 Starch

Anytime Peach Pie

○ Serves 8

> 2 (15-ounce) cans sliced peaches, packed in fruit juice,
>   drained and 1 cup liquid reserved
> 1 (6-ounce) Keebler graham cracker pie crust
> 1 (4-serving) package JELL-O sugar-free vanilla
>   cook-and-serve pudding mix
> 1 (4-serving) package JELL-O sugar-free lemon gelatin
> ½ cup water
> ¾ cup Cool Whip Lite
> 2 tablespoons purchased graham cracker crumbs or
>   2 (2½-inch) graham cracker squares, made into crumbs
> 2 tablespoons chopped pecans
> 2 tablespoons flaked coconut

Evenly arrange peach slices in pie crust. In a medium saucepan, combine dry pudding mix, dry gelatin, reserved peach liquid, and water. Cook over medium heat until mixture thickens and starts to boil, stirring often. Spoon hot mixture evenly over peaches. Refrigerate for at least 2 hours. Evenly spread Cool Whip Lite over set filling. In a small bowl, combine graham cracker crumbs, pecans, and coconut. Sprinkle crumb mixture evenly over top. Refrigerate for at least 10 minutes. Cut into 8 servings.

HINT: A self-seal sandwich bag works great for crushing graham crackers.

Each serving equals:

> HE: 1 Bread • 1 Fruit • ½ Fat • ½ Slider •
> 1 Optional Calorie

> 215 Calories • 7 gm Fat • 2 gm Protein •
> 36 gm Carbohydrate • 248 mg Sodium •
> 2 mg Calcium • 2 gm Fiber

> DIABETIC EXCHANGES: 1 Starch • 1 Fruit • 1 Fat •
> ½ Other Carbohydrate

Pork Plus

Tender Is the Night

It's the title of a famous novel by F. Scott Fitzgerald, but I thought it might make a great name for this menu that treats pork as romantically as Fitzgerald wrote about the glamorous rich! In my opinion, pork deserves more attention than it's often given in other cookbooks. It's available very lean and can be an economical choice for your family dinners.

THE PLAN: Tonight, you'll ready two baking dishes to be cooked simultaneously in a 350 degree oven. My **Sweet Dressing** is the kind of dish you might see only at holiday time, but its fruity goodness is perfect with pork. **Creamy Baked Pork Tenders** must first be browned in the skillet but then go into the oven, topped with a luscious sauce that couldn't be easier to prepare. While these dishes bake for 45 minutes or so, you can simmer a delectable veggie dish, **Good Green Stuff**, and fix a scrumptious dessert—**Chocolate-Cinnamon Creams.** When you're not sure what to serve, "try a little tenderness."

Good Green Stuff

● Serves 4 (1 cup)

> 1 (14-ounce) can Swanson Lower Sodium Fat Free
>   Chicken Broth
> 1 cup chopped onion
> 1 (2.5-ounce) jar sliced mushrooms, drained
> 2½ cups frozen cut green beans, thawed
> 1½ cups frozen chopped broccoli, thawed
> ½ teaspoon lemon pepper
> 1 teaspoon dried parsley flakes

In a large skillet, combine chicken broth, onion, and mushrooms. Stir in green beans and broccoli. Add lemon pepper and parsley flakes. Mix well to combine. Bring mixture to a boil. Lower heat and simmer for 30 minutes or until vegetables are soft and most of liquid is evaporated, stirring occasionally.

HINT: Thaw green beans and broccoli by placing in a colander and rinsing under hot water for 1 minute.

Each serving equals:

HE: 2¾ Vegetable • 8 Optional Calories

---

72 Calories • 0 gm Fat • 5 gm Protein •
13 gm Carbohydrate • 336 mg Sodium •
76 mg Calcium • 4 gm Fiber

DIABETIC EXCHANGES: 3 Vegetable

Sweet Dressing

○ Serves 4

1 cup chopped celery
½ cup finely chopped onion
8 slices reduced-calorie white bread, made into large crumbs
2 tablespoons seedless raisins
1 cup (2 small) cored, peeled, and chopped cooking apples
1 cup unsweetened apple juice
2 tablespoons Splenda Granular
1½ teaspoons apple pie spice

Preheat oven to 350 degrees. Spray an 8-by-8-inch baking dish with butter-flavored cooking spray. In a large skillet sprayed with butter-flavored cooking spray, sauté celery and onion for 6 to 8 minutes. In a large bowl, combine bread crumbs, raisins, and apples. Stir in celery and onion mixture. In a small bowl, combine apple juice, Splenda, and apple pie spice. Add apple juice mixture to bread crumb mixture. Mix well to combine. Pat mixture into prepared baking dish. Cover and bake for 30 minutes. Uncover and continue baking for 10 to 15 minutes. Divide into 4 servings.

Each serving equals:

HE: 1¼ Fruit • 1 Bread • ¾ Vegetable • 3 Optional Calories

---

169 Calories • 1 gm Fat • 6 gm Protein •
34 gm Carbohydrate • 259 mg Sodium •
67 mg Calcium • 1 gm Fiber

DIABETIC EXCHANGES: 1 Fruit • 1 Starch • ½ Vegetable

Creamy Baked Pork Tenders

○ Serves 4

4 (4-ounce) lean pork tenderloins or cutlets
1 (10¾-ounce) can Healthy Request Cream of Mushroom
    Soup
1 tablespoon Land O Lakes no-fat sour cream
1 (2.5-ounce) jar sliced mushrooms, drained
1 tablespoon dried parsley flakes
⅛ teaspoon black pepper

Preheat oven to 350 degrees. Spray an 8-by-8-inch baking dish with butter-flavored cooking spray. In a large skillet sprayed with butter-flavored cooking spray, lightly brown pork for 3 to 4 minutes on each side. Evenly arrange browned meat in prepared baking dish. In a medium bowl, combine mushroom soup, sour cream, mushrooms, parsley flakes, and black pepper. Spoon soup mixture evenly over browned meat. Bake for 40 to 45 minutes. When serving, evenly spoon sauce over top of tenderloins.

HINT: Do not overcook meat when browning as it could become tough.

Each serving equals:

HE: 3 Protein • ¼ Vegetable • ½ Slider •
7 Optional Calories

---

173 Calories • 5 gm Fat • 24 gm Protein •
8 gm Carbohydrate • 428 mg Sodium •
76 mg Calcium • 0 gm Fiber

DIABETIC EXCHANGES: 3 Meat • ½ Other Carbohydrate

Chocolate-Cinnamon Creams

Serves 4

> 1 (4-serving) package JELL-O sugar-free instant chocolate fudge
>   pudding mix
> ⅔ cup Carnation Nonfat Dry Milk Powder
> 1½ cups water
> ½ teaspoon vanilla extract
> ½ teaspoon ground cinnamon
> ¾ cup Dannon plain fat-free yogurt
> ½ cup Cool Whip Free

In a large bowl, combine dry pudding mix, dry milk powder, and water. Mix well using a wire whisk. Blend in vanilla extract and cinnamon. Add yogurt and Cool Whip Free. Mix gently to combine. Evenly spoon mixture into 4 dessert dishes. Refrigerate for at least 15 minutes.

Each serving equals:

HE: ¾ Fat Free Milk • ½ Slider • 10 Optional Calories

108 Calories • 0 gm Fat • 7 gm Protein •
20 gm Carbohydrate • 433 mg Sodium •
244 mg Calcium • 0 gm Fiber

DIABETIC EXCHANGES: 1 Fat Free Milk •
½ Other Carbohydrate

The Pleasures of Pork

Because it has such a delicate flavor of its own, pork is an ideal meat for enriching with an intensely flavorful sauce. And because it's, as the ads say, "the other white meat," a pork meal feels a bit lighter than one featuring beef. Now that the big-box stores sell such beautifully cut meats, you can fill your freezer with these little tenderloins or cutlets and never be at a loss to create a tasty meal.

THE PLAN: This meal is a quickie, with no dish requiring more than about 20 minutes of preparation. Make the **Pistachio Peach Pudding** and rush it into the refrigerator while you move on to **Pork Cacciatore**, which needs some browning of the meat before you make the sauce and then combine them. While your entrée is simmering, you'll make the **Savory Green Beans in Cheese Sauce** and **Sour Cream Noodles.** (Just remember you'll need cooked noodles for that dish.) What a pleasure—a meal that requires so little effort on your part, but delivers such a lot of taste satisfaction and flavor!

Savory Green Beans in Cheese Sauce

⊙ Serves 4 (½ cup)

¾ cup water
¼ cup Land O Lakes Fat Free Half & Half
⅓ cup Carnation Nonfat Dry Milk Powder
1 tablespoon all-purpose flour
¾ cup shredded Kraft reduced-fat Cheddar cheese
1 teaspoon dried onion flakes
⅛ teaspoon black pepper
1 (15-ounce) can cut green beans, rinsed and drained

In a covered jar, combine water, half & half, dry milk powder, and flour. Shake well to blend. Pour milk mixture into a medium saucepan sprayed with butter-flavored cooking spray. Add Cheddar cheese, onion flakes, and black pepper. Mix well to combine. Cook over medium heat for 5 minutes or until mixture thickens and cheese melts, stirring often. Stir in green beans. Continue cooking for 3 to 4 minutes or until mixture is heated through, stirring often.

Each serving equals:

HE: 1 Protein • 1 Vegetable • ¼ Fat Free Milk •
17 Optional Calories

107 Calories • 3 gm Fat • 10 gm Protein •
10 gm Carbohydrate • 463 mg Sodium •
254 mg Calcium • 2 gm Fiber

DIABETIC EXCHANGES: 1 Meat • 1 Vegetable •
½ Other Carbohydrate

Sour Cream Noodles

○ Serves 4 (¾ cup)

½ cup Land O Lakes no-fat sour cream

¼ cup Kraft Reduced Fat Parmesan Style Grated Topping

1 tablespoon dried onion flakes

1 teaspoon dried parsley flakes

¼ teaspoon dried minced garlic

2 teaspoons Worcestershire sauce

2 cups hot cooked noodles, rinsed and drained

In a large skillet sprayed with olive oil–flavored cooking spray, combine sour cream, Parmesan cheese, onion flakes, parsley flakes, garlic, and Worcestershire sauce. Add noodles. Mix well to combine. Cook over medium-low heat for 6 to 8 minutes or until mixture is heated through, stirring occasionally.

HINT: Usually 1¾ cups uncooked noodles cooks to about 2 cups.

Each serving equals:

HE: 1 Bread • ¼ Protein • ¼ Slider •
10 Optional Calories

163 Calories • 3 gm Fat • 5 gm Protein •
29 gm Carbohydrate • 180 mg Sodium •
101 mg Calcium • 1 gm Fiber

DIABETIC EXCHANGES: 1½ Starch •
½ Other Carbohydrate

Pork Cacciatore

● Serves 4

4 (4-ounce) lean pork tenderloins or cutlets
1 cup chopped onion
1 cup chopped green bell pepper
1 (15-ounce) can diced tomatoes, undrained
1 (10¾-ounce) can Healthy Request Tomato Soup
1½ teaspoons Italian seasoning

In a large skillet sprayed with olive oil–flavored cooking spray, lightly brown pork for 3 to 4 minutes on each side. Remove meat to a plate and cover to keep warm. In same skillet, sauté onion and green pepper for 5 to 6 minutes. Stir in undrained tomatoes, tomato soup, and Italian seasoning. Evenly arrange browned pork in sauce mixture. Lower heat, cover, and simmer for 10 minutes or until vegetables and pork are tender. When serving, evenly spoon sauce mixture over pork pieces.

HINT: Do not overcook meat when browning as it could become tough.

Each serving equals:

HE: 3 Protein • 2 Vegetable • ½ Slider •
5 Optional Calories

229 Calories • 5 gm Fat • 25 gm Protein •
21 gm Carbohydrate • 424 mg Sodium •
33 mg Calcium • 3 gm Fiber

DIABETIC EXCHANGES: 3 Meat • 2 Vegetable •
½ Other Carbohydrate

Pistachio Peach Pudding

● Serves 4

1 (4-serving) package JELL-O sugar-free instant
     pistachio pudding mix
⅔ cup Carnation Nonfat Dry Milk Powder
1 cup water
¾ cup Dannon plain fat-free yogurt
½ cup Cool Whip Lite☆
1 (8-ounce) can sliced peaches, packed in fruit juice,
     finely chopped and undrained
2 tablespoons peach spreadable fruit

In a large bowl, combine dry pudding mix, dry milk powder,
and water. Mix well using a wire whisk. Blend in yogurt and ¼ cup
Cool Whip Lite. Add undrained chopped peaches. Mix gently to
combine. Evenly spoon mixture into 4 dessert dishes. In a small
bowl, gently combine spreadable fruit and remaining ¼ cup Cool
Whip Lite. Evenly spoon topping mixture over top of each pudding. Refrigerate for at least 15 minutes.

Each serving equals:

HE: 1 Fruit • ¾ Fat Free Milk • ½ Slider •
5 Optional Calories

---

153 Calories • 1 gm Fat • 7 gm Protein •
29 gm Carbohydrate • 420 mg Sodium •
245 mg Calcium • 1 gm Fiber

DIABETIC EXCHANGES: 1 Fruit • ½ Fat Free Milk •
½ Other Carbohydrate

Sunset Supper

I just love those long summer days, when sunset comes late and you can serve dinner outside on the patio if you like! This is a super-easy skillet meal that will satisfy your taste buds without overstuffing your tummy. As you linger over iced coffee, why not start counting the stars with your loved one in your arms? I can almost guarantee you won't count too many before the evening turns a little romantic!

THE PLAN: If the night is steamy and the humidity high, this meal is just about perfect. You use only the microwave and one stove burner to get dinner ready—what could be better than that? First, make the **Fruit Cocktail Sour Cream Pudding Treats**. They'll be extra-good when they're as cool and creamy as can be. Next, make the **Western Pork Tenders over Rice**, which can simmer on the stove while you wander your flower garden looking for a few perfect blooms. Both your salad and veggie dishes are ready in an instant: **Green Beans with Mushrooms** needs just 2 minutes in the microwave, and **Old-Fashioned Tossed Salad** is just tossed together and served. What a beautiful night, and what a lovely meal to accompany it!

Old-Fashioned Tossed Salad

● Serves 4 (1 cup)

4 cups shredded lettuce
1 cup grated carrots
½ cup chopped radishes
½ cup Kraft Fat Free French Dressing
2 tablespoons Kraft fat-free mayonnaise
1 teaspoon dried onion flakes
1 teaspoon dried parsley flakes

In a large bowl, combine lettuce, carrots, and radishes. In a small bowl, combine French dressing, mayonnaise, onion flakes, and parsley flakes. Drizzle dressing mixture evenly over lettuce mixture. Toss gently to coat. Serve at once.

Each serving equals:

HE: 1¾ Vegetable • ½ Slider • 10 Optional Calories

68 Calories • 0 gm Fat • 1 gm Protein •
16 gm Carbohydrate • 328 mg Sodium •
23 mg Calcium • 3 gm Fiber

DIABETIC EXCHANGES: 1½ Vegetable •
½ Other Carbohydrate

Green Beans with Mushrooms

○ Serves 4 (½ cup)

1 (15-ounce) can cut green beans, rinsed and drained
1 (4-ounce) jar sliced mushrooms, drained
1 teaspoon lemon pepper
1 tablespoon + 1 teaspoon I Can't Believe It's Not Butter! Light
*   Margarine*

In a medium-sized microwaveable glass bowl, combine green beans, mushrooms, lemon pepper, and margarine. Microwave on HIGH (100 percent power) for 2 minutes or until mixture is heated through. Mix well before serving.

Each serving equals:

HE: 1½ Vegetable • ½ Fat

---

50 Calories • 2 gm Fat • 2 gm Protein •
6 gm Carbohydrate • 466 mg Sodium •
26 mg Calcium • 3 gm Fiber

DIABETIC EXCHANGES: 1½ Vegetable • ½ Fat

Western Pork Tenders over Rice

○ Serves 4

4 (4-ounce) lean pork tenderloins or cutlets, each cut into
    1-inch pieces
½ cup chopped green bell pepper
½ cup chopped red bell pepper
1 cup chopped onion
1 (10¾-ounce) can Healthy Request Tomato Soup
1 teaspoon chili seasoning
1 teaspoon dried parsley flakes
⅛ teaspoon black pepper
2 cups hot cooked rice

In a large skillet sprayed with butter-flavored cooking spray, sauté pork, green pepper, red pepper, and onion for 6 to 8 minutes. Stir in tomato soup, chili seasoning, parsley flakes, and black pepper. Lower heat and simmer for 8 to 10 minutes or until pork is tender, stirring occasionally. For each serving, place ½ cup rice on a plate and spoon about ¾ cup meat mixture over top.

HINT: Usually 1⅓ cups uncooked instant rice cooks to about 2 cups.

Each serving equals:

HE: 3 Protein • 1 Bread • 1 Vegetable • ½ Slider •
10 Optional Calories

269 Calories • 5 gm Fat • 25 gm Protein •
31 gm Carbohydrate • 307 mg Sodium •
17 mg Calcium • 2 gm Fiber

DIABETIC EXCHANGES: 3 Meat • 1 Starch •
1 Vegetable • ½ Other Carbohydrate

Fruit Cocktail Sour Cream Pudding Treats

○ Serves 4

1 (4-serving) package JELL-O sugar-free instant vanilla pudding
   mix
⅔ cup Carnation Nonfat Dry Milk Powder
1 (15-ounce) can fruit cocktail, packed in fruit juice,
   drained, and ½ cup liquid reserved
1 cup water
½ cup Land O Lakes no-fat sour cream
2 tablespoons purchased graham cracker crumbs or
   2 (2½-inch) graham cracker squares, made into crumbs

In a medium bowl, combine dry pudding mix, dry milk powder, reserved fruit cocktail juice, and water. Mix well using a wire whisk. Blend in sour cream. Fold in fruit cocktail. Evenly spoon mixture into 4 dessert dishes. Sprinkle 1½ teaspoons graham cracker crumbs over each. Refrigerate for at least 15 minutes.

HINT: A self-seal sandwich bag works great for crushing graham
   crackers.

Each serving equals:

HE: 1 Fruit • ½ Fat Free Milk • ¾ Slider •
4 Optional Calories

---

144 Calories • 0 gm Fat • 5 gm Protein •
31 gm Carbohydrate • 317 mg Sodium •
199 mg Calcium • 1 gm Fiber

DIABETIC EXCHANGES: 1 Fruit • ½ Fat Free Milk •
½ Other Carbohydrate

Bonanza of Flavors

I checked the dictionary, and bonanza means something excessively rich, lush, and rewarding. The word came into wide use to describe the discovery of a quantity of gold or silver worth millions, I found. Well, the notion works for me when I think about this menu, which has elements of all those words. The entrée is both lush and rich in its creaminess; the dessert is jam-packed with rewarding little treats; and knowing that you can enjoy such terrific food while watching your weight, caring for your heart health, or coping with your diabetes has got to be worth millions!

THE PLAN: I like knowing my salad and dessert courses are already ready when I start to prepare my hot dishes, so let's make those first: **Tossed Carrot-Apple Salad** is sweet and colorful, mixes up in a minute, and tastes better when it's chilled. **Butterscotch Bonanzas** are quick and easy, with sweet surprises all through. Next, preheat the oven to 350 degrees and get going on the **Oven Pork Bake with Stuffing**. After you make the stuffing and brown the meat, you're ready to assemble and bake. Finally, you can stir up **Green Beans and Potatoes** on top of the stove. Sis-boom-bah, start the parade—dinner's ready!

Tossed Carrot-Apple Salad

● Serves 4

1½ cups shredded carrots

1 cup (2 small) cored, unpeeled, and finely chopped
    Red Delicious apples

2 tablespoons chopped walnuts

¼ cup Kraft Fat Free French Dressing

1 tablespoon orange marmalade spreadable fruit

4 lettuce leaves

In a medium bowl, combine carrots, apples, and walnuts. Add French dressing and spreadable fruit. Mix gently to combine. Cover and refrigerate for at least 15 minutes. For each salad, place a lettuce leaf on salad plate and spoon a full ½ cup salad mixture over top.

Each serving equals:

HE: ¾ Fruit • ¾ Vegetable • ¼ Fat • ¼ Slider • 11 Optional Calories

90 Calories • 2 gm Fat • 1 gm Protein • 17 gm Carbohydrate • 165 mg Sodium • 18 mg Calcium • 3 gm Fiber

DIABETIC EXCHANGES: 1 Fruit • ½ Vegetable • ½ Fat

Green Beans and Potatoes

○ Serves 4 (full 1 cup)

½ cup finely chopped onion
1¼ cups water
4 cups frozen cut green beans, thawed
2 cups peeled and diced raw potatoes
1 tablespoon + 1 teaspoon I Can't Believe It's Not Butter!
    Light Margarine
1 teaspoon dried parsley flakes
1 teaspoon lemon pepper
1 teaspoon Splenda Granular

In a large skillet sprayed with butter-flavored cooking spray, sauté onion for 5 minutes. Stir in water, green beans, and potatoes. Bring mixture to a boil. Lower heat, cover, and simmer for 20 minutes or just until potatoes are tender. Stir in margarine, parsley flakes, lemon pepper, and Splenda. Continue simmering, uncovered, for 5 minutes or until most of the liquid is absorbed, stirring occasionally.

HINT: Thaw green beans by placing in a colander and rinsing under hot water for one minute.

Each serving equals:

HE: 2¼ Vegetable • ½ Bread • ½ Fat •
1 Optional Calorie

130 Calories • 2 gm Fat • 4 gm Protein •
24 gm Carbohydrate • 170 mg Sodium •
67 mg Calcium • 4 gm Fiber

DIABETIC EXCHANGES: 2 Vegetable • ½ Starch • ½ Fat

Oven Pork Bake with Stuffing

● Serves 4

1 (10¾-ounce) can Healthy Request Cream of Mushroom Soup☆
½ cup water
1 teaspoon dried onion flakes
¼ teaspoon poultry seasoning
½ teaspoon ground sage
⅛ teaspoon black pepper
6 slices reduced-calorie white bread, torn into small pieces
4 (4-ounce) lean pork tenderloins or cutlets

Preheat oven to 350 degrees. Spray an 8-by-8-inch baking dish with butter-flavored cooking spray. In a large bowl, combine ½ cup mushroom soup, water, onion flakes, poultry seasoning, sage, and black pepper. Stir in bread pieces. Evenly spread mixture in prepared baking dish. In a large skillet sprayed with butter-flavored cooking spray, lightly brown pork for 3 to 4 minutes on each side. Evenly arrange browned meat pieces over stuffing mixture. Spoon remaining soup evenly over top. Bake for 30 minutes. Place baking dish on a wire rack and let set for 5 minutes. Divide into 4 servings.

HINT: Do not overcook pork when browning as it could become tough.

Each serving equals:

HE: 3 Protein • ¾ Bread • ½ Slider •
1 Optional Calorie

226 Calories • 6 gm Fat • 27 gm Protein •
16 gm Carbohydrate • 482 mg Sodium •
96 mg Calcium • 0 gm Fiber

DIABETIC EXCHANGES: 3 Meat • 1 Starch •
½ Other Carbohydrate

Butterscotch Bonanzas

⊙ Serves 4

> 1 (4-serving) package JELL-O sugar-free instant butterscotch
>   pudding mix
> ⅔ cup Carnation Nonfat Dry Milk Powder
> 1 cup water
> 1 (8-ounce) can crushed pineapple, packed in fruit juice,
>   undrained
> ½ cup Cool Whip Lite☆
> ½ teaspoon coconut extract
> 2 tablespoons mini chocolate chips
> 1 tablespoon + 1 teaspoon flaked coconut

In a medium bowl, combine dry pudding mix, dry milk powder, water, and undrained pineapple. Mix well using a wire whisk. Blend in ¼ cup Cool Whip Lite and coconut extract. Stir in chocolate chips. Evenly spoon mixture into 4 dessert dishes. Top each with 1 tablespoon Cool Whip Lite and 1 teaspoon coconut. Refrigerate for at least 15 minutes.

Each serving equals:

HE: ½ Fat Free Milk • ½ Fruit • ¾ Slider •
9 Optional Calories

---

118 Calories • 2 gm Fat • 4 gm Protein •
21 gm Carbohydrate • 407 mg Sodium •
160 mg Calcium • 1 gm Fiber

DIABETIC EXCHANGES: ½ Fat Free Milk • ½ Fruit •
½ Other Carbohydrate

Supper in a Jiffy

You've got to love a meal that can be ready to serve in less time than it takes to drive through a fast-food restaurant or wait for a pizza to be delivered! Besides the quick pace, you know you're getting good nutrition, probably saving money, and making time to sit down with your family for dinner. There are plenty of time-saving short-cuts in the kitchen, but the best shortcut of all is having a stockpile of recipes that are fast and easy to prepare!

THE PLAN: **Pistachio Chocolate Dream Pie** is mixed up and ready in minutes to hit the refrigerator. While it chills, the rest of the meal comes together. **Ham and Corn Soup** is soothing, satisfying, and simmers without much attention from you. My **Jiffy Cheese Biscuits** are great for first-time or experienced bakers and taste just great when they're served warm from the oven. Start out with a **Green Salad with French Bacon Dressing,** and you've got a super meal that even Superman could finish before racing off to save the world!

Green Salad with French Bacon Dressing

○ Serves 4

⅓ cup Kraft Fat Free French Dressing
1 tablespoon Kraft fat-free mayonnaise
1 teaspoon dried onion flakes
1 teaspoon dried parsley flakes
¼ cup Oscar Mayer or Hormel Real Bacon Bits
6 cups torn mixed salad greens or shredded lettuce

In a medium bowl, combine French dressing, mayonnaise, onion flakes, and parsley flakes. Stir in bacon bits. For each salad, place 1½ cups salad greens on a salad plate and drizzle about 2 tablespoons dressing mixture over top.

Each serving equals:

HE: 1½ Vegetable • ½ Slider • 10 Optional Calories

74 Calories • 2 gm Fat • 4 gm Protein •
10 gm Carbohydrate • 387 mg Sodium •
59 mg Calcium • 2 gm Fiber

DIABETIC EXCHANGES: 1½ Vegetable • ½ Meat

Ham and Corn Soup

● Serves 4 (1¼ cups)

½ cup chopped onion
1 (10¾-ounce) can Healthy Request Tomato Soup
1 (8-ounce) can stewed tomatoes, undrained
1½ cups diced Dubuque 97% fat-free ham or any extra-lean ham
1½ cups frozen whole-kernel corn, thawed
1 teaspoon dried parsley flakes
⅛ teaspoon black pepper

In a medium saucepan sprayed with butter-flavored cooking spray, sauté onion for 5 minutes. Stir in tomato soup and undrained stewed tomatoes. Add ham, corn, parsley flakes, and black pepper. Mix well to combine. Lower heat and simmer for 6 to 8 minutes or until mixture is heated through, stirring often.

HINT: Thaw corn by placing in a colander and rinsing under hot water for 1 minute.

Each serving equals:

HE: 1½ Protein • ¾ Bread • ¾ Vegetable • ½ Slider • 5 Optional Calories

195 Calories • 3 gm Fat • 14 gm Protein • 28 gm Carbohydrate • 712 mg Sodium • 26 mg Calcium • 3 gm Fiber

DIABETIC EXCHANGES: 1½ Meat • 1 Starch • 1 Vegetable • ½ Other Carbohydrate

Jiffy Cheese Biscuits

◐ Serves 4

¾ cup Bisquick Reduced Fat Baking Mix
½ cup + 1 tablespoon shredded Kraft reduced-fat
  Cheddar cheese
¼ cup fat-free milk
2 tablespoons Land O Lakes no-fat sour cream

Preheat oven to 425 degrees. Spray a baking sheet with butter-flavored cooking spray. In a medium bowl, combine baking mix and Cheddar cheese. Add milk and sour cream. Mix gently just to combine. Drop by tablespoonful to form 4 biscuits. Bake for 10 to 12 minutes or until golden brown. Place baking sheet on a wire rack and let set for 2 to 3 minutes. Serve warm.

Each serving equals:

HE: 1 Bread • ¾ Protein • 13 Optional Calories

132 Calories • 4 gm Fat • 7 gm Protein •
17 gm Carbohydrate • 373 mg Sodium •
156 mg Calcium • 1 gm Fiber

DIABETIC EXCHANGES: 1 Starch • 1 Meat

Pistachio Chocolate Dream Pie

○ Serves 8

> 1 (4-serving) package JELL-O sugar-free instant chocolate
>   pudding mix
> 1⅓ cups Carnation Nonfat Dry Milk Powder☆
> 2¼ cups water☆
> 1 (6-ounce) Keebler graham cracker pie crust
> 1 (4-serving) package JELL-O sugar-free instant pistachio
>   pudding mix
> ½ cup Cool Whip Free
> ½ teaspoon coconut extract
> 2 tablespoons flaked coconut
> 2 tablespoons purchased graham cracker crumbs or
>   2 (2½-inch) graham cracker squares, made into fine crumbs

In a large bowl, combine dry chocolate pudding mix, ⅔ cup dry milk powder, and 1¼ cups water. Mix well using a wire whisk. Spread pudding mixture evenly in pie crust. Refrigerate while preparing topping. In a medium bowl, combine dry pistachio pudding mix, remaining ⅔ cup dry milk powder, and remaining 1 cup water. Mix well using a wire whisk. Blend in Cool Whip Free and coconut extract. Evenly spread topping mixture over set filling. In a small bowl, combine coconut and graham cracker crumbs. Sprinkle crumb mixture evenly over top. Refrigerate for at least 30 minutes. Cut into 8 servings.

HINT: A self-seal sandwich bag works great for crushing graham crackers.

Each serving equals:

HE: 1 Bread • ½ Fat Free Milk • ¼ Fat • ½ Slider •
6 Optional Calories

194 Calories • 6 gm Fat • 6 gm Protein •
29 gm Carbohydrate • 486 mg Sodium •
151 mg Calcium • 1 gm Fiber

DIABETIC EXCHANGES: 1 Starch • 1 Fat •
½ Fat Free Milk • ½ Other Carbohydrate

A Soothing Supper

Sometimes the meals we find most comforting are those that makes us feel like happy kids again. Just think: no bills to pay, no boss to appease, no challenging teenagers to parent, and no aches and pains! Well, I can't take away all those stresses, but maybe I can help you handle them better with this soul-soothing supper that invites you to sit back, relax, and just breathe.

THE PLAN: Since tonight's dinner has two—count 'em, two—desserts, why not start with those? The **Fruit Gelatin Cups** take just a moment to fill but two hours to jell. Done with that? Now it's cookie-baking time! **Cliff's Oatmeal Cookies** are definite man-pleasers, but I've never had a kid turn them down, either. The starter and entrée are both last-minute marvels, so just have the ingredients ready to combine in the fifteen minutes before you want to eat. **Creamed Corn and Ham over Toast** is a substantial skillet supper dish that simmers while you make **Creamy Tomatoes and Cucumbers.** One-two-three, ready or not, it's suppertime!

Creamy Tomatoes and Cucumbers

○ Serves 4 (¾ cup)

> 1½ cups chopped unpeeled cucumbers
> 2 cups chopped unpeeled fresh tomatoes
> ⅓ cup Kraft Fat Free Ranch Dressing
> 2 teaspoons Splenda Granular
> 2 teaspoons dried parsley flakes

In a medium bowl, combine cucumbers and tomatoes. Add ranch dressing, Splenda, and parsley flakes. Mix gently to combine. Cover and refrigerate for 10 minutes. Gently stir again just before serving.

HINT: Do not let vegetables sit in dressing mixture for more than 15 minutes before serving or vegetables will cause dressing to "run."

Each serving equals:

HE: 1¾ Vegetable • ¼ Slider • 13 Optional Calories

52 Calories • 0 gm Fat • 1 gm Protein •
12 gm Carbohydrate • 243 mg Sodium •
17 mg Calcium • 1 gm Fiber

DIABETIC EXCHANGES: 1½ Vegetable

Creamed Corn and Ham over Toast

● Serves 4

½ cup finely diced celery
½ cup chopped onion
1 (8-ounce) can cream-style corn
1 full cup diced Dubuque 97% fat-free ham or any
    extra-lean ham
1 (10¾-ounce) can Healthy Request Cream of Celery Soup
¼ cup Land O Lakes Fat Free Half & Half
1 teaspoon dried parsley flakes
⅛ teaspoon black pepper
4 slices reduced-calorie white bread, toasted

In a large skillet sprayed with butter-flavored cooking spray, sauté celery and onion for 8 minutes. Stir in corn and ham. Add celery soup, half & half, parsley flakes, and black pepper. Mix well to combine. Lower heat and simmer for 5 minutes, stirring often. When serving, place 1 piece of toast on a plate and spoon about ¾ cup ham mixture over top.

Each serving equals:

HE: 1 Bread • 1 Protein • ½ Vegetable • ½ Slider • 11 Optional Calories

195 Calories • 3 gm Fat • 12 gm Protein • 30 gm Carbohydrate • 824 mg Sodium • 116 mg Calcium • 1 gm Fiber

DIABETIC EXCHANGES: 1 Starch • 1 Meat • ½ Vegetable • ½ Other Carbohydrate

Fruit Gelatin Cups

⚪ Serves 4

1 (4-serving) package JELL-O sugar-free strawberry gelatin
1 cup boiling water
1 (15-ounce) can fruit cocktail, packed in fruit juice, drained
    and ½ cup liquid reserved
¼ cup cold water
¼ cup Cool Whip Lite

In a large bowl, combine dry gelatin and boiling water. Mix well to dissolve gelatin. Stir in reserved fruit cocktail liquid and cold water. Evenly spoon fruit cocktail into 4 (12-ounce) custard cups. Carefully spoon gelatin mixture evenly over fruit. Refrigerate until firm, about 2 hours. When serving, top each with 1 table-spoon Cool Whip Lite.

Each serving equals:

HE: 1 Fruit • 14 Optional Calories

60 Calories • 0 gm Fat • 1 gm Protein •
14 gm Carbohydrate • 9 mg Sodium •
9 mg Calcium • 1 gm Fiber

DIABETIC EXCHANGES: 1 Fruit

Cliff's Oatmeal Cookies

◑ Serves 8 (2 each)

1 cup all-purpose flour
1 cup quick oats
½ cup Splenda Granular
½ teaspoon table salt
½ teaspoon baking powder
½ teaspoon baking soda
½ teaspoon ground cinnamon
2 eggs or equivalent in egg substitute
¼ cup I Can't Believe It's Not Butter! Light Margarine
2 teaspoons vanilla extract
½ cup seedless raisins

Preheat oven to 350 degrees. Spray 2 baking sheets with butter-flavored cooking spray. In a large bowl, combine flour, oats, Splenda, salt, baking powder, baking soda, and cinnamon. Add eggs, margarine, and vanilla extract. Mix well just to combine. Fold in raisins. Drop by tablespoonful onto prepared baking sheet to form 16 cookies. Bake for 8 to 10 minutes or just until firm. DO NOT OVERBAKE. Place baking sheets on wire racks and let set for 5 minutes. Remove cookies and continue cooling on wire racks.

Each serving equals:

HE: 1 Bread • ¾ Fat • ½ Fruit • ¼ Protein • 18 Optional Calories

---

169 Calories • 5 gm Fat • 5 gm Protein • 26 gm Carbohydrate • 320 mg Sodium • 38 mg Calcium • 2 gm Fiber

---

DIABETIC EXCHANGES: 1 Starch • 1 Fat • ½ Fruit

I Hope It's Hash!

So much of the pleasure we take in food comes from the big A—anticipation! We let our minds wander through the heaven we imagine the meal to be, skipping through a dish of ice cream, wading through a pool of creamy Alfredo sauce. The more you anticipate a good meal, the harder it may be to please you, but the more likely you are to enjoy it with all your senses! Here's a menu inspired by the kind of hash that puts a smile on your face.

THE PLAN: **Golden Harvest Salad** is a delectable and colorful gelatin dish that requires about two hours in the fridge, though you can certainly make it ahead. Before you serve it, you'll make the creamy, crunchy topping. Your splendid dessert, **Coconut-Pecan Snack Cake,** needs just under half an hour in the oven, so do that next. Now it's time to tackle two skillet dishes, **Glory Bean Side Dish** and the delightful **Stove Top Ham Hash.** Both are ready in little more than fifteen minutes. Wow, what do you know? Dinner is ready and I'm all aglow.

Golden Harvest Salad

○ Serves 4

1 (4-serving) package JELL-O sugar-free orange gelatin
1 cup boiling water
1 (8-ounce) can crushed pineapple, packed in fruit juice,
    undrained
1 cup grated carrots
⅓ cup Kraft fat-free mayonnaise
6 tablespoons shredded Kraft reduced-fat Cheddar cheese
1 tablespoon chopped pecans

In a large bowl, combine dry gelatin and boiling water. Mix well to dissolve gelatin. Stir in undrained pineapple and carrots. Evenly spoon into 4 (6-ounce) custard cups. Refrigerate for at least 2 hours or until firm. In a small bowl, combine mayonnaise and Cheddar cheese. Top each salad with a full 2 tablespoons mayonnaise mixture. Evenly garnish each with ¾ teaspoon pecans. Serve at once or refrigerate until ready to serve.

Each serving equals:

HE: ½ Protein • ½ Fruit • ½ Vegetable • ¼ Fat •
18 Optional Calories

95 Calories • 3 gm Fat • 3 gm Protein •
14 gm Carbohydrate • 243 mg Sodium •
87 mg Calcium • 2 gm Fiber

DIABETIC EXCHANGES: ½ Meat • ½ Fruit •
½ Vegetable

Glory Bean Side Dish

○ Serves 4 (¾ cup)

½ cup diced onion

1 (15-ounce) can cut green beans, rinsed and drained

1 (15-ounce) can cut wax beans, rinsed and drained

2 tablespoons Oscar Mayer or Hormel Real Bacon Bits

¼ cup reduced-sodium ketchup

1 tablespoon apple cider vinegar

1 tablespoon Splenda Granular

In a large skillet sprayed with butter-flavored cooking spray, sauté onion for 6 to 8 minutes. Add green beans, wax beans, and bacon bits. Mix well to combine. Stir in ketchup, vinegar, and Splenda. Lower heat and simmer for 5 minutes or until mixture is heated through, stirring occasionally.

Each serving equals:

HE: 2¼ Vegetable • ¼ Slider • 12 Optional Calories

77 Calories • 1 gm Fat • 4 gm Protein •
13 gm Carbohydrate • 605 mg Sodium •
42 mg Calcium • 3 gm Fiber

DIABETIC EXCHANGES: 2 Vegetable

Stove Top Ham Hash

◐ Serves 4 (1 cup)

1 cup chopped onion
2 full cups diced cooked potatoes
1½ cups diced Dubuque 97% fat-free ham or any
    extra-lean ham
⅓ cup Land O Lakes Fat Free Half & Half
1½ teaspoons dried parsley flakes
⅛ teaspoon black pepper

In a large skillet sprayed with butter-flavored cooking spray, sauté onion and potatoes for 8 to 10 minutes. Stir in ham. Add half & half, parsley flakes, and black pepper. Mix well to combine. Lower heat, cover, and simmer for 5 to 6 minutes, stirring occasionally.

Each serving equals:

HE: 1½ Protein • ¾ Bread • ½ Vegetable •
13 Other Carbohydrate •

170 Calories • 2 gm Fat • 14 gm Protein •
24 gm Carbohydrate • 506 mg Sodium •
45 mg Calcium • 2 gm Fiber

DIABETIC EXCHANGES: 1½ Meat • 1 Starch •
½ Vegetable

Coconut-Pecan Snack Cake

○ Serves 8

1½ cups Bisquick Reduced Fat Baking Mix
1¼ cups Splenda Granular☆
1 teaspoon baking powder
1 egg or equivalent in egg substitute
¼ cup Land O Lakes no-fat sour cream
½ cup fat-free milk
1 teaspoon coconut extract
¼ cup Land O Lakes Fat Free Half & Half
1 teaspoon ground cinnamon
¼ cup flaked coconut
¼ cup chopped pecans

Preheat oven to 350 degrees. Spray a 9-inch round cake pan with butter-flavored cooking spray. In a large bowl, combine baking mix, ¾ cup Splenda, and baking powder. Add egg, sour cream, milk, and coconut extract. Mix gently just to combine. Spread batter into prepared pan. In a small bowl, combine half & half, remaining ½ cup Splenda, and cinnamon. Stir in coconut and pecans. Evenly spoon mixture over cake batter. Bake for 20 to 24 minutes or until cake tests done in center. Place pan on a wire rack and allow to cool. Cut into 8 servings.

Each serving equals:

HE: 1 Bread • ½ Fat • ½ Slider • 2 Optional Calories

157 Calories • 5 gm Fat • 4 gm Protein •
24 gm Carbohydrate • 301 mg Sodium •
106 mg Calcium • 1 gm Fiber

DIABETIC EXCHANGES: 1 Starch • 1 Fat •
½ Other Carbohydrate

A Taste of Italy

I couldn't write a cookbook without at least one luscious, scrumptious, impossibly creamy, utterly dreamy Alfredo recipe, so that beloved Italian classic is at the heart of this menu! It's a beautiful-looking dish, the aromatic sauce enrobing the pasta, tossed in lovely swirls upon your plate. (It's also one of my quickest meals to prepare!) Perhaps that is why so much great art has come from Italy, and so much spectacular music, too. When the food is inspiring, the work just naturally improves. Hmm, I must try eating this menu when I've got a speech to write or a newsletter to create!

THE PLAN: It's a toss-up, really, to decide what recipes should be first in line. Everything is very speedy tonight! Well, even though the Italians traditionally eat salad after the main course, let's start with **Roman Tossed Salad** and chill the mixture while you make the rest of the meal. Done? Good. Now cook and drain your pasta so you can take the next step. In one skillet get the **Italian Broccoli Side Dish** going, and in the second start the **Creamy Fettuccine Ham Alfredo.** Both are done in just a few minutes. Get your dessert ingredients ready, because you'll be making that right before serving. **Taste of Italy Shortcakes** are a lovely way to end this meal. *Arrivederci, Roma!*

Roman Tossed Salad

○ Serves 4 (1½ cups)

6 cups torn mixed salad greens
1 cup cherry tomatoes
1 cup chopped fresh mushrooms
½ cup Kraft Fat Free Italian Dressing
2 tablespoons Splenda Granular
½ teaspoon dried basil

In a large bowl, combine salad greens, tomatoes, and mushrooms. In a small bowl, combine Italian dressing, Splenda, and basil. Drizzle dressing mixture evenly over greens mixture. Toss gently to combine. Cover and refrigerate for 15 minutes. Gently toss again, just before serving.

Each serving equals:

HE: 2½ Vegetable • 17 Optional Calories

48 Calories • 0 gm Fat • 3 gm Protein •
9 gm Carbohydrate • 404 mg Sodium •
68 mg Calcium • 3 gm Fiber

DIABETIC EXCHANGES: 2 Vegetable

Italian Broccoli Side Dish

○ Serves 4 (½ cup)

1 (10-ounce) package frozen chopped broccoli, thawed
¼ cup reduced-sodium ketchup
1 tablespoon white distilled vinegar
1 tablespoon Splenda Granular
½ teaspoon Italian seasoning
¼ cup Kraft Reduced Fat Parmesan Style Grated Topping

In a large skillet sprayed with butter-flavored cooking spray, sauté broccoli for 5 minutes. Stir in ketchup, vinegar, Splenda, and Italian seasoning. Add Parmesan cheese. Mix well to combine. Lower heat and simmer for 3 to 4 minutes or until mixture is heated through, stirring occasionally.

HINT: Thaw broccoli by placing in a colander and rinsing under hot water for 1 minute.

Each serving equals:

HE: ½ Vegetable • ¼ Protein • 16 Optional Calories

65 Calories • 1 gm Fat • 3 gm Protein •
11 gm Carbohydrate • 126 mg Sodium •
88 mg Calcium • 2 gm Fiber

DIABETIC EXCHANGES: ½ Vegetable •
½ Other Carbohydrate

Creamy Fettuccine
Ham Alfredo

⊙ Serves 4 (½ cup)

½ cup Land O Lakes no-fat sour cream
1 tablespoon + 1 teaspoon I Can't Believe It's Not Butter! Light
    Margarine
¼ cup Land O Lakes Fat Free Half & Half
¼ cup Kraft Reduced Fat Parmesan Style Grated Topping
1 teaspoon dried parsley flakes
⅛ teaspoon black pepper
2 cups hot cooked fettuccine, rinsed and drained
1 full cup diced Dubuque 97% fat-free ham or any
    extra-lean ham

In a large skillet sprayed with butter-flavored cooking spray, combine sour cream, margarine, half & half, Parmesan cheese, parsley flakes, and black pepper. Cook over medium heat for 2 minutes. Stir in fettuccine and ham. Continue cooking for 2 to 3 minutes or until mixture is heated through, stirring often.

HINT: Usually 1½ cups uncooked fettuccine cooks to about
    2 cups.

Each serving equals:

HE: 1¼ Protein • 1 Bread • ½ Fat • ½ Slider

201 Calories • 5 gm Fat • 13 gm Protein •
26 gm Carbohydrate • 482 mg Sodium •
115 mg Calcium • 1 gm Fiber

DIABETIC EXCHANGES: 1 Meat • 1 Starch • ½ Fat •
½ Other Carbohydrate

Taste of Italy Shortcakes

● Serves 4

> 1 (4-serving) package JELL-O sugar-free instant pistachio
>   pudding mix
> ⅔ cup Carnation Nonfat Dry Milk Powder
> 1½ cups water
> ¼ cup Cool Whip Free
> 4 individual sponge cake dessert cups
> 1 cup Wells' Blue Bunny sugar- and fat-free vanilla ice cream
>   or any sugar- and fat-free ice cream
> 2 maraschino cherries, halved

In a medium bowl, combine dry pudding mix, dry milk powder, and water. Mix well using a wire whisk. Gently blend in Cool Whip Free. For each shortcake, place 1 sponge cake in a dessert dish, arrange ¼ cup ice cream over dessert cup, spoon about ½ cup pistachio mixture over top, and garnish with 1 cherry half. Serve at once.

Each serving equals:

HE: 1 Bread • ¾ Fat Free Milk • ¾ Slider •
3 Optional Calories

---

218 Calories • 2 gm Fat • 8 gm Protein •
42 gm Carbohydrate • 542 mg Sodium •
230 mg Calcium • 1 gm Fiber

DIABETIC EXCHANGES: 2 Other Carbohydrate •
1 Fat Free Milk

Paradise at Dinner

Wherever you find pineapple, you find paradise—that's just how it works. The glorious sun required to sweeten this magnificent fruit also produces the most gorgeous foliage in the world, along with warm temperatures and tropical breezes. So since this meal features that superstar of fruits, the queen of paradise, I chose that name for this menu. Try this experiment: Take a piece of pineapple and place it softly on your tongue. Close your lips and breathe in the flavor. Let it melt in your mouth. There, did you get a glimpse of paradise? I thought so!

THE PLAN: First into the oven is **Pineapple Ham Loaf**, which requires about an hour to bake. (Remember, for best results your ham needs to be ground, so you'll need to use a food processor or grinder at home, or ask the butcher for help.) Dessert tonight is **Pineapple Pudding Cake**, which can be made in advance or simultaneously if you have a double oven. Allow just over a half hour to make it and let it cool. **Cheesy Green Beans and Corn Side Dish** is a stovetop sensation, ready in just a few minutes, and your **Lettuce Salad with Crisp Relish Dressing** should be prepared just before you ring the dinner bell. Paradise is calling—don't be late!

Lettuce Salad with Crisp Relish Dressing

◑ Serves 6

6 cups shredded lettuce
1 cup shredded carrots
½ cup finely chopped red radishes
½ cup Kraft fat-free mayonnaise
¼ cup sweet pickle relish
2 tablespoons white distilled vinegar

In a large bowl, combine lettuce, carrots, and radishes. In a small bowl, combine mayonnaise, pickle relish, and vinegar. For each serving, place 1 full cup lettuce mixture on a salad plate and spoon a full 2 tablespoons dressing mixture over top. Serve at once.

Each serving equals:

HE: 1½ Vegetable • ¼ Slider • 5 Optional Calories

40 Calories • 0 gm Fat • 1 gm Protein • 9 gm Carbohydrate • 205 mg Sodium • 17 mg Calcium • 2 gm Fiber

DIABETIC EXCHANGES: 1½ Vegetable

Cheesy Green Beans and Corn Side Dish

○ Serves 6 (full ½ cup)

1 (10¾-ounce) can Healthy Request Cream of Mushroom Soup
¾ cup cubed Velveeta Light processed cheese
1 teaspoon dried onion flakes
1 teaspoon dried parsley flakes
⅛ teaspoon black pepper
3 cups frozen cut green beans, thawed
1½ cups frozen whole-kernel corn, thawed

In a medium saucepan, combine mushroom soup, Velveeta cheese, onion flakes, parsley flakes, and black pepper. Stir in green beans and corn. Lower heat and simmer for 8 to 10 minutes or until cheese is melted and green beans are tender, stirring often.

HINT: Thaw green beans and corn by placing in a colander and rinsing under hot water for 1 minute.

Each serving equals:

HE: 1 Vegetable • ½ Bread • ½ Protein • ¼ Slider • 8 Optional Calories

123 Calories • 3 gm Fat • 5 gm Protein • 19 gm Carbohydrate • 404 mg Sodium • 151 mg Calcium • 3 gm Fiber

DIABETIC EXCHANGES: 1 Vegetable • ½ Starch • ½ Meat • ½ Other Carbohydrate

Pineapple Ham Loaf

● Serves 6

4½ cups ground Dubuque 97% fat-free ham or any extra-lean
    ham
½ cup + 1 tablespoon purchased graham cracker crumbs or
    9 (2½-inch) graham cracker squares, made into crumbs
½ cup finely chopped onion
¼ cup finely chopped green bell pepper
1 (8-ounce) can crushed pineapple, packed in fruit juice,
    drained
¼ cup reduced-sodium ketchup

Preheat oven to 350 degrees. Spray a 9-by-5-inch loaf pan
with butter-flavored cooking spray. In a large bowl, combine ham,
cracker crumbs, onion, green pepper, pineapple, and ketchup. Mix
well to combine. Pat mixture into prepared loaf pan. Bake for 50 to
60 minutes. Place loaf pan on a wire rack and let set for 5 minutes.
Divide into 6 servings.

HINTS: 1. If you don't have a grinder, ask your butcher to grind
        ham.
      2. A self-seal sandwich bag works great for crushing gra-
        ham crackers.

Each serving equals:

HE: 2⅔ Protein • ½ Bread • ⅓ Fruit • ¼ Vegetable •
10 Optional Calories

192 Calories • 4 gm Fat • 20 gm Protein •
19 gm Carbohydrate • 802 mg Sodium •
13 mg Calcium • 1 gm Fiber

DIABETIC EXCHANGES: 3 Meat • ½ Starch •
½ Other Carbohydrate

Pineapple Pudding Cake

○ Serves 6

1 cup + 2 tablespoons
　　Bisquick Reduced Fat
　　Baking Mix
½ cup Splenda Granular
1 teaspoon baking powder
½ cup fat-free milk
1 (8-ounce) can crushed
　　pineapple, packed in
　　fruit juice, undrained

2 tablespoons I Can't Believe
　　It's Not Butter! Light
　　Margarine
½ teaspoon coconut extract
3 tablespoons chopped pecans
1 cup Diet Mountain Dew
½ cup unsweetened orange
　　juice
2 tablespoons flaked coconut

Preheat oven to 350 degrees. Spray 6 (8-ounce) custard cups with butter-flavored cooking spray. In a large bowl, combine baking mix, Splenda, and baking powder. Add milk, undrained pineapple, and margarine. Mix well to combine. Fold in coconut extract and pecans. Evenly spoon batter into prepared custard cups. In a medium saucepan, combine Diet Mountain Dew and orange juice. Heat mixture until just to boiling point. Evenly pour about ¼ cup hot mixture over each "cake." Sprinkle 1 teaspoon coconut over top of each. Place custard cups on a baking sheet. Bake for 20 to 24 minutes. Place custard cups on a wire rack and let set for at least 10 minutes.

HINT: Good warm with sugar- and fat-free ice cream or cold with Cool Whip Free. If using either, count calories accordingly.

Each serving equals:

HE: 1 Bread • 1 Fat • ½ Fruit • ¼ Slider • 1 Optional Calorie

178 Calories • 6 gm Fat • 3 gm Protein • 28 gm Carbohydrate • 337 mg Sodium • 104 mg Calcium • 1 gm Fiber

DIABETIC EXCHANGES: 1 Starch • 1 Fat • ½ Fruit

A Marvelous Maple Meal

Our nation has been favored with abundant maple trees, which is a good thing, because Americans have always loved the intensely sweet taste of maple syrup. Most of us think of maple syrup coming from New England more than anywhere else in the country, and many of the most delicious products and delightful recipes using maple flavor come from that region. But maple belongs to all of us, and this menu gives us two scrumptious chances to revel in its special sweetness!

THE PLAN: Our starter tonight is **Calico Perfection Salad,** a citrusy gelatin salad that is oh-so-very refreshing. It must be made at least three hours before you expect to serve dinner, but you can certainly make it the night before. Now, about an hour before dinner, mix up **Maple Raisin Cheesecake** and allow it to chill. Next, you'll fix the **Maple Sweet Potato Bake,** which needs about thirty minutes overall. Finally, your entrée, **Orange Glazed Ham,** warms up sweet and luscious in the oven for about fifteen minutes before serving. S'wonderful, S'marvelous, as the song goes—and this meal certainly is!

Calico Perfection Salad

○ Serves 6

1 (4-serving) package JELL-O sugar-free lemon gelatin
1 cup boiling water
½ cup cold water
¼ cup cider vinegar
2 cups finely shredded cabbage
1 cup chopped celery
1 (2-ounce) jar chopped pimiento, drained

In a large bowl, combine dry gelatin and boiling water. Mix well to dissolve gelatin. Stir in cold water and vinegar. Add cabbage, celery, and pimiento. Mix well to combine. Pour mixture into an 8-by-8-inch dish. Refrigerate until firm, about 3 hours. Cut into 6 servings.

Each serving equals:

HE: ⅔ Vegetable • 4 Optional Calories

16 Calories • 0 gm Fat • 1 gm Protein •
3 gm Carbohydrate • 27 mg Sodium •
23 mg Calcium • 1 gm Fiber

DIABETIC EXCHANGES: Free Food

Maple Sweet Potato Bake

● Serves 6

1 (18-ounce) can vacuum-packed sweet potatoes
¼ cup Log Cabin Sugar Free Maple Syrup
2 tablespoons Splenda Granular
3 tablespoons chopped pecans
2 tablespoons I Can't Believe It's Not Butter! Light Margarine

Preheat oven to 350 degrees. Spray an 8-by-8-inch baking dish with butter-flavored cooking spray. Thinly slice sweet potatoes and arrange in prepared baking dish. In a small bowl, combine maple syrup, Splenda, and pecans. Drizzle syrup mixture evenly over sweet potatoes. Drop margarine by teaspoon to form 6 mounds. Bake for 20 to 25 minutes. Place baking dish on a wire rack and let set for 5 minutes. Divide into 6 servings.

Each serving equals:

HE: 1 Bread • 1 Fat • 7 Optional Calories

129 Calories • 5 gm Fat • 2 gm Protein •
19 gm Carbohydrate • 107 mg Sodium •
22 mg Calcium • 2 gm Fiber

DIABETIC EXCHANGES: 1 Starch • 1 Fat

Orange Glazed Ham

○ Serves 6

> 6 (3-ounce) slices Dubuque 97% fat-free ham or any
>   extra-lean ham
> 6 tablespoons orange marmalade spreadable fruit
> 1 tablespoon Splenda Granular
> 2 tablespoons Diet Mountain Dew
> 1 teaspoon dried onion flakes
> 1 teaspoon dried parsley flakes

Preheat oven to 350 degrees. Spray an 8-by-12-inch baking dish with butter-flavored cooking spray. Evenly arrange ham slices in prepared baking dish. In a small bowl, combine spreadable fruit, Splenda, Diet Mountain Dew, onion flakes, and parsley flakes. Spread mixture evenly over ham slices. Bake for 15 minutes or until ham is heated through.

HINT: A 3-ounce slice of ham is usually about ⅓ inch thick.

Each serving equals:

HE: 2 Protein • 1 Fruit • 1 Optional Calorie

122 Calories • 2 gm Fat • 14 gm Protein •
12 gm Carbohydrate • 609 mg Sodium •
1 mg Calcium • 0 gm Fiber

DIABETIC EXCHANGES: 2 Meat • 1 Fruit

Maple Raisin Cheesecake

○ Serves 8

> 2 (8-ounce) packages Philadelphia fat-free cream cheese
> 1 (4-serving) package JELL-O sugar-free instant vanilla pudding mix
> ⅔ cup Carnation Nonfat Dry Milk Powder
> 1 cup water
> ¾ cup Cool Whip Free☆
> 1 cup seedless raisins
> 1 (6-ounce) Keebler graham cracker piecrust
> ¼ cup Log Cabin Sugar Free Maple Syrup
> 1 tablespoon purchased graham cracker crumbs or 1 (2½-inch)
>   graham cracker square, made into crumbs

In a large bowl, stir cream cheese with a sturdy spoon until soft. Add dry pudding mix, dry milk powder, and water. Mix well using a wire whisk. Fold in ¼ cup Cool Whip Free and raisins. Spread mixture evenly into piecrust. In a small bowl, gently combine remaining ½ cup Cool Whip Free and maple syrup. Evenly spread topping mixture over cream cheese mixture. Sprinkle graham cracker crumbs evenly over top. Refrigerate for at least 1 hour. Cut into 8 servings.

HINT: A self-seal sandwich bag works great for crushing graham crackers.

Each serving equals:

HE: 1 Bread • 1 Protein • 1 Fruit • ¼ Fat Free Milk • ¼ Fat • ¼ Slider • 10 Optional Calories

253 Calories • 5 gm Fat • 13 gm Protein • 39 gm Carbohydrate • 603 mg Sodium • 244 mg Calcium • 1 gm Fiber

DIABETIC EXCHANGES: 1 Starch • 1 Meat • ½ Fat • ½ Other Carbohydrate

Corned Beef Beauty

Is it March 17, the feast of St. Patrick, or are you brave enough to serve corned beef on any other day of the year? I hope you are, because once a year just isn't often enough for a dish that so many have come to love. It's part of my Irish heritage, but even if the only green thing about you is your eyes or your front lawn, it doesn't matter a bit. Corned beef has a taste all its own, and it's worthy of its own menu in this collection. I can't promise that eating it often will bring you the "luck of the Irish" but you never know!

THE PLAN: My husband just loves tapioca, so I always try to include a couple of recipes that feature its old-fashioned goodness in every book I write. Start then with **Creamy Tapioca** and set it to chill before you make the rest of your meal. Next, with love from Iowa, it's **Heart of America Corn Chowder,** which only takes about fifteen minutes from stove to table. While it heats through, make **Corned Beef Sandwich Bake,** maybe the best grilled-cheese-and-meat sandwich you'll ever eat! Finally, **Lunchtime Salad** whips up in seconds for a crunchy, fresh first course. From one Irish cook to another (honorary or not)!

Lunchtime Salad

○ Serves 4

6 cups shredded lettuce
1 cup chopped fresh tomato
½ cup Kraft Fat Free Italian Dressing
½ cup coarsely crushed French's Original Fried Onions

In a large bowl, combine lettuce and tomato. Add Italian dressing. Mix gently just to combine. For each salad, place a full 1½ cups lettuce mixture on a salad plate and sprinkle 2 tablespoons onions over top. Serve at once.

Each serving equals:

HE: 2 Vegetable • ½ Slider • 13 Optional Calories

79 Calories • 3 gm Fat • 2 gm Protein •
11 gm Carbohydrate • 454 mg Sodium •
76 mg Calcium • 2 gm Fiber

DIABETIC EXCHANGES: 2 Vegetable •
½ Other Carbohydrate

Heart of America
Corn Chowder

⚫ Serves 4 (1 cup)

½ cup finely chopped onion
¼ cup Oscar Mayer or Hormel Real Bacon Bits
1 (10¾-ounce) can Healthy Request Cream of Celery Soup
1 (12-fluid-ounce) can Carnation Evaporated Fat Free Milk
1½ cups frozen whole-kernel corn, thawed
¾ cup diced cooked potatoes

In a medium saucepan sprayed with butter-flavored cooking spray, sauté onion for 5 minutes. Stir in bacon bits. Add celery soup, evaporated milk, corn, and potatoes. Mix well to combine. Lower heat and simmer for 10 minutes, stirring occasionally.

HINT: Thaw corn by placing in a colander and rinsing under hot water for 1 minute.

Each serving equals:

HE: 1 Bread • ¾ Fat Free Milk • ¼ Vegetable •
¾ Slider • 6 Optional Calories

191 Calories • 3 gm Fat • 10 gm Protein •
31 gm Carbohydrate • 514 mg Sodium •
272 mg Calcium • 2 gm Fiber

DIABETIC EXCHANGES: 1 Starch • 1 Fat Free Milk •
½ Meat • ½ Other Carbohydrate

Corned Beef Sandwich Bake

● Serves 4

4 slices reduced-calorie white bread, toasted
2 (2.5-ounce) packages Carl Buddig 90% lean corned beef,
    shredded
¼ cup Kraft fat-free mayonnaise
2 teaspoons prepared yellow mustard
¼ cup sliced ripe olives
4 (¼-inch) slices ripe tomato
4 (¾-ounce) slices Kraft reduced-fat Cheddar cheese

Preheat oven to 425 degrees. Spray a baking sheet with butter-flavored cooking spray. Evenly arrange toasted bread slices on prepared baking sheet. In a medium bowl, combine corned beef, mayonnaise, mustard, and olives. Spread about ¼ cup corned beef mixture over each slice of toast. Bake for 8 minutes. Place 1 tomato slice and 1 Cheddar cheese slice on top of each. Continue baking for 2 to 3 minutes or until cheese melts. Serve at once.

Each serving equals:

HE: 2¼ Protein • ½ Bread • ¼ Fat • ¼ Vegetable •
10 Optional Calories

179 Calories • 7 gm Fat • 15 gm Protein •
14 gm Carbohydrate • 941 mg Sodium •
174 mg Calcium • 1 gm Fiber

DIABETIC EXCHANGES: 2 Meat • 1 Other Carbohydrate

Creamy Tapioca

⊙ Serves 4

1 (4-serving) package JELL-O sugar-free vanilla
    cook-and-serve pudding mix
⅔ cup Carnation Nonfat Dry Milk Powder
2½ cups water
¼ cup Quick Cooking Minute Tapioca
½ cup Cool Whip Lite

In a medium saucepan, combine dry pudding mix, dry milk powder, and water. Stir in tapioca. Let set 5 minutes. Cook over medium heat until mixture thickens and starts to boil, stirring constantly. Place saucepan on a wire rack and allow to cool completely, stirring occasionally. When cooled, fold in Cool Whip Lite. Evenly spoon mixture into 4 dessert dishes. Refrigerate for at least 30 minutes.

Each serving equals:

HE: ½ Fat Free Milk • ½ Bread • ¼ Slider

117 Calories • 1 gm Fat • 4 gm Protein •
23 gm Carbohydrate • 171 mg Sodium •
150 mg Calcium • 0 gm Fiber

DIABETIC EXCHANGES: 1 Other Carbohydrate •
½ Fat Free Milk

Entertaining: Sunday Dinners and Celebration Meals

A Special Sunday Sitdown for Four

Sunday dinner is one of my favorite meals of the week, especially when Cliff and I get to share our meal with loved ones. Though often it's just the two of us (and so we have great leftovers), we look forward to dining with our children and grandchildren. This menu features so many of our favorite foods—a crunchy slaw, terrific veggie side dishes of peas and carrots, ovenbaked potatoes, old-fashioned tangy chicken, and a sensational cheesecake for dessert. From our house to your house, with warmth and affection, enjoy this family meal with us!

THE PLAN: With six dishes to make instead of four, it's a good idea to prepare what you can ahead of time. In this case, that's my **Sunday Slaw** and my **Sunday Best Cheesecake,** which will do just fine in your fridge while you cook up everything else. Now you need to get the **Cheesy Hash Brown Potatoes** and **Grandma's Baked Chicken** ready for the oven. The potatoes are just mixed and baked; the chicken requires dipping and dredging to coat before being baked. Each takes about forty-five minutes to cook. Two saucepans on the stove get the **Special Peas** and **Classy Carrots Side Dish** going. Both need fifteen to twenty minutes of sautéeing and simmering. It can seem a challenge to get all the dishes ready at the same time, but I know you can do it so everyone gets to sit down together and visit.

Sunday Slaw

⚫ Serves 4 (¾ cup)

⅓ cup Carnation Nonfat Dry Milk Powder
¼ cup water
1 tablespoon white distilled vinegar
1 tablespoon lemon juice
¼ cup Splenda Granular
¼ cup Kraft fat-free mayonnaise
1 teaspoon dried parsley flakes
⅛ teaspoon black pepper
3 cups very finely chopped cabbage
½ cup shredded carrots

In a large bowl, combine dry milk powder, water, vinegar, lemon juice, and Splenda. Let set for 5 minutes. Add mayonnaise, parsley flakes, and black pepper. Mix well to combine. Stir in cabbage and carrots. Cover and refrigerate for at least 1 hour. Gently stir again just before serving.

Each serving equals:

HE: 1 Vegetable • ¼ Fat Free Milk •
16 Optional Calories

60 Calories • 0 gm Fat • 3 gm Protein •
12 gm Carbohydrate • 168 mg Sodium •
112 mg Calcium • 2 gm Fiber

DIABETIC EXCHANGES: 1 Vegetable •
½ Other Carbohydrate

Special Peas

○ Serves 4 (½ cup)

½ cup finely chopped onion
1 (2.5-ounce) jar sliced mushrooms, undrained
2 cups frozen peas, thawed
⅛ teaspoon black pepper
2 teaspoons I Can't Believe It's Not Butter! Light Margarine

In a medium saucepan sprayed with butter-flavored cooking spray, sauté onion for 5 minutes or until tender. Stir in undrained mushrooms, peas, and black pepper. Add margarine. Mix well to combine. Lower heat and simmer for 10 minutes or until most of liquid is absorbed, stirring occasionally.

Each serving equals:

HE: 1 Bread • ½ Vegetable • ¼ Fat

73 Calories • 1 gm Fat • 4 gm Protein •
12 gm Carbohydrate • 186 mg Sodium •
22 mg Calcium • 4 gm Fiber

DIABETIC EXCHANGES: 1 Starch

Classy Carrots Side Dish

○ Serves 4 (½ cup)

½ cup finely chopped onion
½ cup finely chopped green bell pepper
1 (10¾-ounce) can Healthy Request Tomato Soup
⅛ teaspoon black pepper
3 cups frozen sliced carrots, thawed

In a large skillet sprayed with butter-flavored cooking spray, sauté onion and green pepper for 6 to 8 minutes or until tender. Stir in tomato soup and black pepper. Add carrots. Mix well to combine. Lower heat, cover, and simmer for 8 to 10 minutes or until carrots are tender, stirring occasionally.

HINT: Thaw carrots by placing in a colander and rinsing under hot water for 1 minute.

Each serving equals:

HE: 2 Vegetable • ½ Slider • 5 Optional Calories

105 Calories • 1 gm Fat • 2 gm Protein •
22 gm Carbohydrate • 340 mg Sodium •
36 mg Calcium • 4 gm Fiber

DIABETIC EXCHANGES: 2 Vegetable •
½ Other Carbohydrate

Cheesy Hash Brown Potatoes

● Serves 4

½ cup Land O Lakes no-fat sour cream
⅓ cup Carnation Nonfat Dry Milk Powder
¼ cup water
1 tablespoon dried parsley flakes
4½ cups shredded loose-packed frozen potatoes
1 cup finely chopped onion
1 (2-ounce) jar chopped pimiento, drained
1 teaspoon lemon pepper
1 cup diced Velveeta Light processed cheese

Preheat oven to 350 degrees. Spray an 8-by-8-inch baking dish with butter-flavored cooking spray. In a large bowl, combine sour cream, dry milk powder, water, and parsley flakes. Add potatoes, onion, pimiento, and black pepper. Mix well to combine. Stir in Velveeta cheese. Evenly spread mixture into prepared baking dish. Cover with foil and bake for 30 minutes. Uncover and continue baking for 15 minutes. Place baking dish on a wire rack and let set for 5 minutes. Divide into 4 servings.

HINT: Mr. Dell's frozen shredded potatoes are a good choice or raw shredded potatoes, rinsed and patted dry, may be used in place of frozen potatoes.

Each serving equals:

HE: 1 Protein • ¾ Bread • ½ Vegetable •
¼ Fat Free Milk • ¼ Slider • 10 Optional Calories

195 Calories • 3 gm Fat • 12 gm Protein •
30 gm Carbohydrate • 348 mg Sodium •
276 mg Calcium • 3 gm Fiber

DIABETIC EXCHANGES: 1 Meat • 1 Starch •
½ Vegetable • ½ Other Carbohydrate

Grandma's Baked Chicken

🍂 Serves 4

½ cup Kraft Fat Free Ranch Dressing
1 tablespoon dried onion flakes
2 teaspoons dried parsley flakes
½ cup crushed cornflakes
16 ounces skinned and boned uncooked chicken breast,
*   cut into 4 pieces*

Preheat oven to 350 degrees. Spray an 8-by-8-inch baking dish with butter-flavored cooking spray. In a flat dish, combine ranch dressing, onion flakes, and parsley flakes. Place crushed cornflakes in a saucer. Dip chicken pieces first in dressing mixture, then roll in cornflakes. Place coated chicken pieces in prepared baking dish. Top with any remaining cornflakes, then drizzle any remaining dressing mixture on cornflakes over top of chicken pieces. Bake for 35 to 40 minutes or until chicken is thoroughly cooked. Place baking dish on a wire rack and let set 5 minutes.

Each serving equals:

HE: 3 Protein • ½ Bread • ½ Slider •
8 Optional Calories

203 Calories • 3 gm Fat • 24 gm Protein •
20 gm Carbohydrate • 428 mg Sodium •
23 mg Calcium • 0 gm Fiber

DIABETIC EXCHANGES: 3 Meat • ½ Starch •
½ Other Carbohydrate

Sunday Best Cheesecake

● Serves 8

2 (8-ounce) packages Philadelphia fat-free cream cheese
1 (4-serving) package JELL-O sugar-free instant vanilla
    pudding mix
⅔ cup Carnation Nonfat Dry Milk Powder
1 cup water
¾ cup Cool Whip Free☆
1 teaspoon almond extract☆
1 (6-ounce) Keebler graham cracker piecrust
1 (20-ounce) can Lucky Leaf No Sugar Added
    Cherry Pie Filling
2 tablespoons slivered almonds

In a large bowl, stir cream cheese with a sturdy spoon until soft. Add dry pudding mix, dry milk powder, and water. Mix well using a wire whisk. Gently blend in ¼ cup Cool Whip Free and ½ teaspoon almond extract. Spread mixture evenly into piecrust. In a small bowl, gently combine cherry pie filling, remaining ½ cup Cool Whip Free, and remaining ½ teaspoon almond extract. Evenly spread mixture over cream cheese mixture. Sprinkle almonds evenly over top. Refrigerate for at least 1 hour. Cut into 8 servings.

Each serving equals:

HE: 1 Bread • 1 Protein • ½ Fruit • ½ Fat •
¼ Fat Free Milk • ¼ Slider • 7 Optional Calories

230 Calories • 6 gm Fat • 12 gm Protein •
32 gm Carbohydrate • 603 mg Sodium •
239 mg Calcium • 1 gm Fiber

DIABETIC EXCHANGES: 1 Starch • 1 Meat • 1 Fat •
½ Fruit • ½ Other Carbohydrate

An Old-Fashioned Family Get-Together for Six

Your family evolves and changes, getting smaller and larger at different times in your life. At one time, Sunday dinner meant just my three kids and I. At another, Cliff and I were alone together. And nowadays, with my children living closer and my grandkids getting bigger (and better at traveling), our house sometimes seems to overflow with people and joy! Whatever the makeup of your family (and even if your family is made up of you with your dearest friends), sharing a festive meal together is an important way to acknowledge that these relationships are precious to you. Here's a menu that I hope will appeal to families everywhere.

THE PLAN: With a big meal, I always ask myself, what can do in advance to ease my way? Today, it's **Bountiful Carrot Cake**, which I'll bake ahead and frost when I serve it. I'll also make **Red Raspberry Delight Salad**, at least three hours earlier but likely before I go to bed the night before. Now for the main event: **Apple-Smothered Pork Loins!** I'll brown the meat and make the sauce; after that, it bakes for forty minutes, giving me time to do all the rest. I'll get my **Mixed Vegetable Deluxe** into the saucepan; I'll stir up the **Rustic Mashed Potatoes**; and I'll prepare **Spinach and Mushroom Salad** but not dress it until about ten minutes before serving. Don't be afraid to ask for a little help from your family or friends. They'll enjoy joining you in the kitchen more than you know!

Red Raspberry Delight Salad

○ Serves 6

2 (4-serving) packages JELL-O sugar-free raspberry gelatin
1 cup boiling water
1 (8-ounce) can crushed pineapple, packed in fruit juice,
    undrained
1½ cups Wells' Blue Bunny sugar- and fat-free vanilla ice cream
    or any sugar- and fat-free ice cream
3 cups frozen unsweetened raspberries, slightly thawed

In a large bowl, combine dry gelatin and boiling water. Mix well to dissolve gelatin. Stir in undrained pineapple. Add ice cream. Mix until well blended. Fold in raspberries. Spoon mixture into an 8-by-8-inch dish. Refrigerate until firm, about 3 hours. Cut into 6 servings.

Each serving equals:

HE: 1 Fruit • ¼ Fat Free Milk • ¼ Slider •
7 Optional Calories

---

92 Calories • 0 gm Fat • 4 gm Protein •
19 gm Carbohydrate • 62 mg Sodium •
79 mg Calcium • 4 gm Fiber

DIABETIC EXCHANGES: 1 Fruit • ½ Other Carbohydrate

Spinach and Mushroom Salad

◗ Serves 6 (1 full cup)

6 cups torn fresh spinach leaves, stems removed and discarded
1½ cups chopped fresh mushrooms
¾ cup Kraft Fat Free Italian Dressing
1 tablespoon Splenda Granular
½ teaspoon prepared yellow mustard
3 hard-boiled eggs, cut into large pieces

In a large bowl, combine spinach and mushrooms. In a small bowl, combine Italian dressing, Splenda, and mustard. Drizzle dressing mixture evenly over spinach mixture. Toss well to coat. Cover and refrigerate for at least 10 minutes before serving. Gently stir again just before serving. When serving, evenly top each salad with egg pieces.

Each serving equals:

HE: 1½ Vegetable • ½ Protein • 17 Optional Calories

71 Calories • 3 gm Fat • 5 gm Protein •
6 gm Carbohydrate • 429 mg Sodium •
57 mg Calcium • 1 gm Fiber

DIABETIC EXCHANGES: 1 Vegetable • ½ Meat

Mixed Vegetable Deluxe

○ Serves 6 (⅔ cup)

2 (10-ounce) packages frozen mixed vegetables, thawed
1 tablespoon Splenda Granular
2 tablespoons I Can't Believe It's Not Butter! Light Margarine
2 tablespoons chopped fresh parsley or 2 teaspoons
    dried parsley flakes
1 teaspoon lemon pepper
¼ cup water

In a medium saucepan, combine vegetables, Splenda, margarine, parsley, lemon pepper, and water. Cook over medium heat for 15 minutes or just until vegetables are tender and most of liquid has evaporated, stirring occasionally.

HINT: Thaw vegetables by placing in a colander and rinsing under hot water for 1 minute.

Each serving equals:

HE: 1 Vegetable • ½ Fat • 1 Optional Calorie

78 Calories • 2 gm Fat • 3 gm Protein •
12 gm Carbohydrate • 127 mg Sodium •
26 mg Calcium • 4 gm Fiber

DIABETIC EXCHANGES: 1 Vegetable • ½ Fat

Rustic Mashed Potatoes

○ Serves 6 (¾ cup)

> 5 cups unpeeled and diced raw potatoes
> 3 cups hot water
> ¼ cup Land O Lakes Fat Free Half & Half
> 2 tablespoons I Can't It's Not Butter! Light Margarine
> 1 teaspoon dried parsley flakes
> ½ teaspoon table salt
> ⅛ teaspoon black pepper

In a large saucepan, combine potatoes and water. Cook over medium heat for 15 to 20 minutes or until potatoes are tender. Drain well. Return potatoes to saucepan. Mash potatoes with potato masher or electric mixer. Add half & half, margarine, parsley flakes, salt, and black pepper. Mix gently to combine until potatoes are light and fluffy.

Each serving equals:

HE: 1 Bread • ½ Fat • 7 Optional Calories

106 Calories • 2 gm Fat • 2 gm Protein •
20 gm Carbohydrate • 223 mg Sodium •
22 mg Calcium • 2 gm Fiber

DIABETIC EXCHANGES: 1 Starch • ½ Fat

Apple-Smothered Pork Loins

● Serves 6

6 (4-ounce) lean pork
    tenderloins or cutlets
1½ cups (3 small) cored,
    peeled, and diced tart
    apples
3 tablespoons Log Cabin Sugar
    Free Maple Syrup

1 cup water
1 tablespoon apple cider
    vinegar
3 tablespoons all-purpose flour
6 tablespoons seedless raisins
¼ teaspoon apple pie spice

Preheat oven to 350 degrees. Spray an 8-by-12-inch baking dish with butter-flavored cooking spray. In a large skillet sprayed with butter-flavored cooking spray, lightly brown pork for 3 to 4 minutes on both sides. Evenly arrange browned pork in prepared baking dish. Arrange diced apples evenly over pork. Drizzle maple syrup evenly over apples. In a covered jar, combine water, vinegar, and flour. Shake well to blend. Pour mixture into same skillet pork was browned in. Cook over medium heat until mixture thickens and starts to boil, stirring constantly. Stir in raisins and apple pie spice. Spoon hot mixture evenly over top. Cover and bake for 40 minutes. Uncover and continue baking for 10 minutes. Place baking dish on a wire rack and let set for 5 minutes. When serving, evenly spoon sauce mixture over meat pieces.

HINT: Do not overcook meat when browning as it could become tough.

Each serving equals:

HE: 3 Protein • 1 Fruit • ¼ Slider

197 Calories • 5 gm Fat • 23 gm Protein •
15 gm Carbohydrate • 58 mg Sodium •
12 mg Calcium • 1 gm Fiber

DIABETIC EXCHANGES: 3 Meat • 1 Fruit

Bountiful Carrot Cake

● Serves 8

1 cup Splenda Granular

¼ cup unsweetened applesauce

¼ cup I Can't Believe It's Not Butter! Light Margarine

2 eggs, beaten, or equivalent in egg substitute

1½ cups Bisquick Reduced Fat Baking Mix

1 teaspoon baking powder

1 teaspoon ground cinnamon

2 cups finely grated carrots

¾ cup seedless raisins

2 tablespoons chopped pecans

½ cup Cool Whip Lite

Preheat oven to 350 degrees. Spray a 9-inch round cake pan with butter-flavored cooking spray. In a large bowl, combine Splenda, applesauce, margarine, and eggs. Add baking mix, baking powder, and cinnamon. Mix well just to combine. Fold in carrots, raisins, and pecans. Spread batter evenly into prepared pan. Bake for 30 to 35 minutes or until cake tests done in center. Place pan on a wire rack and allow to cool completely. Cut into 8 wedges. When serving, top each with 1 tablespoon Cool Whip Lite.

Each serving equals:

HE: 1 Bread • 1 Fruit • 1 Fat • ½ Vegetable • ¼ Protein • ¼ Slider • 5 Optional Calories

219 Calories • 7 gm Fat • 4 gm Protein • 35 gm Carbohydrate • 417 mg Sodium • 82 mg Calcium • 2 gm Fiber

DIABETIC EXCHANGES: 1 Starch • 1 Fruit • 1 Fat • ½ Vegetable • ½ Other Carbohydrate

Sensational Salads and Slaw:
An Iowa Backyard Potluck for Eight

It's one of the main reasons we look forward to summer—the chance to invite friends and family to gather in the backyard for a cookout or potluck! Loads of fresh vegetables and fruits are in season, the days are long, and the night sky features a million stars. It's the time of year when cooks all over the Midwest start to stir up all kinds of salads and slaws because they just can't help themselves—and neither can I! This festive menu offers some of my favorite ways to celebrate all summer long.

THE PLAN: When you're planning a big meal like this one, you need to prioritize and make as much ahead of time as possible. **Luscious Lemon Pineapple Salad** is one of those recipes; so are **Backyard Slaw** and my **Just Plain Good Potato Salad.** I almost always make desserts in advance, and this menu is no exception. My **Rocky Road Cake Brownies** and **Mom's Caramel Apple Pie Deluxe** both do just fine when prepared a day or two before your potluck. That leaves three dishes to cook—one in a skillet and two in the oven. All can be reheated without concern, so do them as you wish. I'd probably start with **Potluck Meat Loaf**, which needs about an hour in the oven and some time to set. **Broccoli-Cauliflower-Carrot Bake** requires forty-five minutes in the oven, and my **Old-Fashioned Three-Bean Pot** takes about thirty minutes on your stovetop. Each dish serves eight, but I'd recommend either a taste of everything or regular servings of two side dishes, one entrée, and one dessert.

Luscious Lemon Pineapple Salad

● Serves 8

1 (4-serving) package JELL-O
   sugar-free lemon gelatin
1 cup boiling water
2 (8-ounce) cans crushed
   pineapple, packed in
   fruit juice, undrained☆
1 cup cold water☆
1 (4-serving) package JELL-O
   sugar-free instant vanilla
   pudding mix

⅔ cup Carnation Nonfat Dry
   Milk Powder
½ cup Cool Whip Free
½ teaspoon coconut
   extract
2 tablespoons chopped
   pecans
2 tablespoons flaked coconut

In a large bowl, combine dry gelatin and boiling water. Mix well to dissolve gelatin. Add 1 can undrained pineapple and ½ cup water. Mix well to combine. Pour mixture into an 8-by-8-inch dish. Refrigerate until firm, about 3 hours. In a large bowl, combine dry pudding mix, dry milk powder, remaining can undrained pineapple, and remaining ½ cup cold water. Mix well using a wire whisk. Gently blend in Cool Whip Free and coconut extract. Spread topping mixture evenly over set gelatin. Evenly sprinkle pecans and coconut over top. Refrigerate for at least 15 minutes. Divide into 8 servings.

Each serving equals:

HE: ½ Fruit • ¼ Fat Free Milk • ¼ Fat • ¼ Slider •
9 Optional Calories

90 Calories • 2 gm Fat • 2 gm Protein •
16 gm Carbohydrate • 202 mg Sodium •
84 mg Calcium • 1 gm Fiber

DIABETIC EXCHANGES: ½ Fruit • ½ Fat •
½ Other Carbohydrate

Backyard Slaw

● Serves 8 (¾ cup)

¾ cup Kraft fat-free mayonnaise
2 tablespoons Land O Lakes Fat Free Half & Half
1 tablespoon white distilled vinegar
1½ teaspoons prepared yellow mustard
2 tablespoons Splenda Granular
6 cups purchased coleslaw mix

In a large bowl, combine mayonnaise, half & half, vinegar, mustard, and Splenda. Add coleslaw mix. Mix well to combine. Cover and refrigerate for at least 30 minutes. Gently stir again just before serving.

HINT: 5 cups shredded cabbage and 1 cup shredded carrots may be used in place of purchased coleslaw mix.

Each serving equals:

HE: ¾ Vegetable • 18 Optional Calories

40 Calories • 0 gm Fat • 2 gm Protein •
8 gm Carbohydrate • 189 mg Sodium •
38 mg Calcium • 2 gm Fiber

DIABETIC EXCHANGES: 1 Vegetable

Just Plain Good Potato Salad

☉ Serves 8 (1 cup)

1½ cups Kraft fat-free mayonnaise

2 tablespoons white distilled vinegar

2 tablespoons Splenda Granular

⅛ teaspoon black pepper

2 teaspoons dried parsley flakes

1½ cups diced celery

½ cup chopped onion

4¾ cups diced cold cooked potatoes

2 hard-boiled eggs, chopped

In a large bowl, combine mayonnaise, vinegar, Splenda, black pepper, and parsley flakes. Add celery, onion, and potatoes. Mix well to combine. Gently fold in chopped eggs. Cover and refrigerate for at least 30 minutes. Gently stir again just before serving.

Each serving equals:

HE: ¾ Bread • ½ Vegetable • ¼ Protein • ¼ Slider • 11 Optional Calories

139 Calories • 3 gm Fat • 3 gm Protein • 25 gm Carbohydrate • 369 mg Sodium • 25 mg Calcium • 3 gm Fiber

DIABETIC EXCHANGES: 1 Starch • ½ Vegetable • ½ Other Carbohydrate

Broccoli-Cauliflower-Carrot Bake ❄

○ Serves 8

1 (16-ounce) package frozen broccoli, cauliflower,
    and carrot blend, thawed
1 (10¾-ounce) can Healthy Request Cream of Mushroom
    Soup
¼ cup Land O Lakes no-fat sour cream
¾ cup shredded Kraft reduced-fat Cheddar cheese☆
1 tablespoon dried onion flakes
⅛ teaspoon black pepper
20 Ritz Reduced Fat Crackers, made into crumbs

Preheat oven to 350 degrees. Spray an 8-by-12-inch baking dish with butter-flavored cooking spray. In a large bowl, combine thawed vegetables, mushroom soup, sour cream, ½ cup Cheddar cheese, onion flakes, and black pepper. Evenly spread mixture into prepared baking dish. In a small bowl, combine cracker crumbs and remaining ¼ cup Cheddar cheese. Evenly sprinkle crumb mixture over top. Lightly spray crumb mixture with butter-flavored cooking spray. Bake for 40 to 45 minutes. Place baking dish on a wire rack and let set for 5 minutes. Divide into 8 servings.

HINTS: 1. 1 cup frozen broccoli, 1 cup frozen cauliflower, and 1 cup frozen carrots may be used in place of blended vegetables.
2. Thaw frozen vegetables by placing in a colander and rinsing under hot water for 1 minute.
3. A self-seal sandwich bag works great for crushing crackers.

Each serving equals:

HE: ¾ Vegetable • ½ Bread • ½ Protein • ¼ Slider •
8 Optional Calories

---

108 Calories • 4 gm Fat • 5 gm Protein •
13 gm Carbohydrate • 332 mg Sodium •
140 mg Calcium • 2 gm Fiber

DIABETIC EXCHANGES: 1 Vegetable • 1 Starch • ½ Meat

Old-Fashioned Three-Bean Pot

○ Serves 8 (¾ cup)

1 cup finely chopped onion
1 (8-ounce) can Hunt's Tomato Sauce
1 (8-ounce) can tomatoes, finely chopped and undrained
½ cup Splenda Granular
1 teaspoon prepared yellow mustard
⅛ teaspoon black pepper
1 (15-ounce) can butter or lima beans, rinsed and drained
1 (15-ounce) can red kidney beans, rinsed and drained
1 (15-ounce) can pinto beans, rinsed and drained
¼ cup Oscar Mayer or Hormel Real Bacon Bits

In a large skillet sprayed with butter-flavored cooking spray, sauté onion for 5 minutes. Stir in tomato sauce, undrained tomatoes, Splenda, mustard, and black pepper. Add butter beans, kidney beans, pinto beans, and bacon bits. Mix well to combine. Lower heat and simmer for 20 to 30 minutes, stirring occasionally.

Each serving equals:

HE: 1½ Protein • 1 Vegetable • ½ Bread •
12 Optional Calories

133 Calories • 1 gm Fat • 8 gm Protein •
23 gm Carbohydrate • 508 mg Sodium •
49 mg Calcium • 6 gm Fiber

DIABETIC EXCHANGES: 1 Meat • 1 Vegetable • 1 Starch

Potluck Meat Loaf

● Serves 8

32 ounces extra-lean ground sirloin beef or turkey breast
¾ cup dried fine bread crumbs
1 cup finely chopped celery
1 cup finely chopped onion
¼ cup reduced-sodium ketchup
1 (12-ounce) jar Heinz Fat Free Beef Gravy☆
1 tablespoon dried parsley flakes

Preheat oven to 350 degrees. Spray an 8-by-8-inch baking dish with butter-flavored cooking spray. In a large bowl, combine meat, bread crumbs, celery, onion, ketchup, and ¼ cup beef gravy. Pat mixture evenly into prepared baking dish. Bake for 40 minutes. Stir parsley flakes into remaining gravy. Evenly spoon gravy mixture over partially baked meat loaf. Continue baking for 15 to 20 minutes. Place baking dish on a wire rack and let set for 5 minutes. Divide into 8 servings.

Each serving equals:

HE: 3 Protein • ½ Bread • ½ Vegetable •
19 Optional Calories

197 Calories • 5 gm Fat • 24 gm Protein •
14 gm Carbohydrate • 405 mg Sodium •
35 mg Calcium • 1 gm Fiber

DIABETIC EXCHANGES: 3 Meat • ½ Starch •
½ Vegetable

Mom's Caramel Apple Pie Deluxe

☻ Serves 8

1 Pillsbury refrigerated unbaked 9-inch piecrust
1 (4-serving) package JELL-O sugar-free vanilla cook-and-serve
    pudding mix
1 cup unsweetened apple juice
¼ cup Smucker's Fat Free Caramel Syrup
1½ teaspoons apple pie spice
¼ cup chopped walnuts
4 cups (8 small) cored, peeled, and sliced cooking apples

Preheat oven to 350 degrees. Let piecrust set at room temperature for 10 minutes. Meanwhile, in a medium saucepan, combine dry pudding mix and apple juice. Cook over medium heat until mixture thickens, stirring often. Remove from heat. Stir in caramel syrup, apple pie spice, and walnuts. Cut the pie crust in half on the folded line. Gently roll each half into a ball. Wipe counter with a wet cloth and place a sheet of waxed paper over damp spot. Place one of the balls on the waxed paper. Cover with another piece of waxed paper and roll out into a 9-inch circle with a rolling pin. Carefully remove waxed paper from one side and place crust into an 8-inch pie plate. Remove other piece of waxed paper. Arrange apple slices in prepared piecrust. Evenly spoon pudding mixture over apples. Repeat process of rolling out remaining piecrust half. Place second crust over top of pie and flute edges. Make about 8 slashes with a knife to allow steam to escape. Bake for 50 to 55 minutes. Place pie plate on a wire rack and allow to cool completely. Cut into 8 servings.

HINT: Place piece of uncooked elbow macaroni upright in center of pie to act as a "chimney" to keep the filling from cooking out of crust.

Each serving equals:

HE: 1¼ Fruit • 1 Bread • ¾ Fat • ¼ Slider •
15 Optional Calories

---

221 Calories • 9 gm Fat • 1 gm Protein •
34 gm Carbohydrate • 186 mg Sodium •
17 mg Calcium • 2 gm Fiber

DIABETIC EXCHANGES: 1 Fruit • 1 Starch • 1 Fat •
½ Other Carbohydrate

Rocky Road Cake Brownies

🟤 Serves 8 (2 each)

1½ cups Bisquick Reduced Fat Baking Mix

¾ cup Splenda Granular

¼ cup unsweetened cocoa powder

⅓ cup Land O Lakes no-fat sour cream

2 tablespoons + 2 teaspoons I Can't Believe It's Not Butter! Light Margarine

1 egg or equivalent in egg substitute

¾ cup water

2 teaspoons vanilla extract

1 cup miniature marshmallows

¼ cup mini chocolate chips

¼ cup chopped walnuts

Preheat oven to 350 degrees. Spray a 9-by-13-inch cake pan with butter-flavored cooking spray. In a large bowl, combine baking mix, Splenda, and cocoa. Add sour cream, margarine, egg, water, and vanilla extract. Mix well using a sturdy spoon. Spread batter into prepared cake pan. Bake for 10 minutes. Evenly sprinkle marshmallows over top of partially baked brownies. In a small bowl, combine chocolate chips and walnuts. Sprinkle mixture evenly over marshmallows. Continue baking for 5 minutes or until a toothpick inserted in center comes out clean. Place cake pan on a wire rack and allow to cool completely. Cut into 16 brownies.

Each serving equals:

HE: 1 Bread • ¾ Fat • ¼ Protein • ¾ Slider • 2 Optional Calories

195 Calories • 7 gm Fat • 4 gm Protein • 29 gm Carbohydrate • 301 mg Sodium • 48 mg Calcium • 2 gm Fiber

DIABETIC EXCHANGES: 1 Starch • 1 Fat • 1 Other Carbohydrate

Sunny Summer Garden Party for Six

I wish you could see my garden in person this summer. It's going to be magnificent, fragrant, and colorful as only the Iowa summer sun can produce! Its beauties feed my soul as satisfyingly as my recipes feed our tummies. I've got a lovely patio for backyard parties here at Timber Ridge Farm, but sometimes I'm tempted to set up a couple of picnic tables and a gas grill closer to the garden, so we can feast our eyes and noses on nature at the same time we're eating up a storm. Who knows, maybe this summer I will!

THE PLAN: Because I like to spend my time visiting with my guests instead of all alone in the kitchen, I'll prepare my salads ahead of time. Today, I'm featuring **Fruit Cocktail Pistachio Fluff Salad**, just as pretty as it sounds, and **Come and Get It Macaroni Salad**, a wonderfully creamy classic. I've also got another version of that family favorite, **Continental Three-Bean Salad.** I'll probably fix a batch of **Backyard "Wine" Punch** to offer everyone when they arrive. So all that's left is my luscious **Grilled Pork with Summer Fruit Salsa** (you can make it on an outdoor grill or an electric one inside) and **Strawberry Romanoff Coconut Cobbler**, a truly delectable dessert sure to please all.

Fruit Cocktail
Pistachio Fluff Salad

○ Serves 6 (⅔ cup)

> 1 (4-serving) package JELL-O sugar-free instant pistachio
>   pudding mix
> ⅔ cup Carnation Nonfat Dry Milk Powder
> 1 cup water
> 1 (15-ounce) can fruit cocktail, packed in fruit juice, drained and
>   ⅓ cup liquid reserved
> ¾ cup Cool Whip Free
> 1 cup (1 medium) diced banana
> ½ cup miniature marshmallows

In a large bowl, combine dry pudding mix and dry milk powder. Add water and reserved fruit cocktail liquid. Mix well using a wire whisk. Blend in Cool Whip Free. Fold in fruit cocktail, banana, and marshmallows. Cover and refrigerate for at least 30 minutes. Gently stir again just before serving.

Each serving equals:

HE: 1 Fruit • ⅓ Fat Free Milk • ½ Slider •
8 Optional Calories

124 Calories • 0 gm Fat • 3 gm Protein •
28 gm Carbohydrate • 235 mg Sodium •
107 mg Calcium • 1 gm Fiber

DIABETIC EXCHANGES: 1 Fruit • 1 Other Carbohydrate

Come and Get It Macaroni Salad

○ Serves 6 (½ cup)

¾ cup Kraft fat-free mayonnaise
2 tablespoons Land O Lakes no-fat sour cream
¼ cup sweet pickle relish
1½ teaspoons prepared yellow mustard
1 teaspoon Splenda Granular
⅛ teaspoon black pepper
1 (2-ounce) jar chopped pimiento, drained
2½ cups cooked elbow macaroni, rinsed and drained
½ cup frozen peas, thawed

In a large bowl, combine mayonnaise, sour cream, pickle relish, mustard, Splenda, and black pepper. Add pimiento, macaroni, and peas. Mix well to combine. Cover and refrigerate for at least 30 minutes. Gently stir again just before serving.

HINTS: 1. Usually 1⅔ cups uncooked elbow macaroni cooks to about 2½ cups.
2. Thaw peas by placing in a colander and rinsing under hot water for one minute.

Each serving equals:

HE: 1 Bread • ¼ Slider • 15 Optional Calories

128 Calories • 0 gm Fat • 4 gm Protein •
28 gm Carbohydrate • 348 mg Sodium •
15 mg Calcium • 2 gm Fiber

DIABETIC EXCHANGES: 1 Starch •
½ Other Carbohydrate

Continental Three-Bean Salad

○ Serves 6 (⅔ cup)

1 (15-ounce) can cut green beans, rinsed and drained
1 (15-ounce) can wax beans, rinsed and drained
1 (15-ounce) can great northern beans, rinsed and drained
½ cup chopped red onion
2 tablespoons Kraft Fat Free Italian Dressing
¼ cup Kraft Fat Free French Dressing
2 tablespoons chopped fresh parsley or 2 teaspoons dried
    parsley flakes

In a large bowl, combine green beans, wax beans, great northern beans, and red onion. Add Italian dressing, French dressing,
and parsley. Mix well to combine. Cover and refrigerate for at least
30 minutes. Gently stir again just before serving.

Each serving equals:

HE: 1½ Vegetable • ½ Protein • ¼ Bread •
¼ Slider • 19 Optional Calories

76 Calories • 0 gm Fat • 3 gm Protein •
16 gm Carbohydrate • 503 mg Sodium •
45 mg Calcium • 5 gm Fiber

DIABETIC EXCHANGES: 1½ Vegetable • ½ Meat •
½ Starch

Grilled Pork with Summer Fruit Salsa

● Serves 6

2 cups diced fresh strawberries
1½ cups (3 medium) peeled and diced fresh peaches
1 cup (2 medium) peeled and diced kiwifruit
1 tablespoon lemon juice
1 tablespoon lime juice
2 tablespoons Splenda Granular

½ teaspoon ground ginger
2 tablespoons apricot spreadable fruit
6 tablespoons Kraft Fat Free Catalina Dressing
6 (4-ounce) lean pork tenderloins or cutlets

In a medium bowl, combine strawberries, peaches, and kiwifruit. Add lemon juice, lime juice, Splenda, and ginger. Mix well to combine. Cover and refrigerate for at least 30 minutes to allow flavors to blend. When ready to grill, in a shallow saucepan, combine spreadable fruit and Catalina dressing. Spray grill with butter-flavored cooking spray. Evenly coat tenderloins on both sides in dressing mixture. Place tenderloins on prepared grill. Drizzle any remaining dressing mixture evenly over top of tenderloins. Grill tenderloins over medium heat for 4 to 5 minutes on each side or until pork is no longer pink. When serving, top each tenderloin with about ½ cup fruit salsa.

HINT: A double-sided electric grill may be used in place of outdoor grill.

Each serving equals:

HE: 3 Protein • 1½ Fruit • 19 Optional Calories

208 Calories • 4 gm Fat • 23 gm Protein • 20 gm Carbohydrate • 206 mg Sodium • 23 mg Calcium • 3 gm Fiber

DIABETIC EXCHANGES: 3 Meat • 1½ Fruit

Strawberry Romanoff Coconut Cobbler

◐ Serves 6

4 cups chopped fresh strawberries

1 (4-serving) package JELL-O sugar-free vanilla cook-and-serve pudding mix

1 cup unsweetened orange juice

1 cup + 2 tablespoons Bisquick Reduced Fat Baking Mix

2 tablespoons Splenda Granular

½ cup Land O Lakes Fat Free Half & Half

2 tablespoons Land O Lakes no-fat sour cream

1½ teaspoons coconut extract

3 tablespoons flaked coconut

Preheat oven to 400 degrees. Spray an 8-by-8-inch baking dish with butter-flavored cooking spray. Evenly arrange strawberries in prepared baking dish. In a medium saucepan, combine dry pudding mix and orange juice. Cook over medium heat until mixture thickens and starts to boil, stirring often. Drizzle hot mixture evenly over strawberries. In a large bowl, combine baking mix and Splenda. Add half & half, sour cream, and coconut extract. Mix gently just to combine. Spread batter evenly over fruit. Evenly sprinkle coconut over top. Bake for 25 to 30 minutes. Place baking dish on a wire rack and let set for 5 minutes. Divide into 6 servings.

Each serving equals:

HE: 1 Bread • 1 Fruit • ½ Slider • 4 Optional Calories

175 Calories • 3 gm Fat • 4 gm Protein •
33 gm Carbohydrate • 327 mg Sodium •
80 mg Calcium • 3 gm Fiber

DIABETIC EXCHANGES: 1 Starch • 1 Fruit •
½ Other Carbohydrate

Backyard "Wine" Punch

○ Serves 6 (¾ cup)

1 cup cold diet ginger ale
1 (8-ounce) can crushed pineapple, packed in fruit juice,
    undrained
¼ cup Splenda Granular
2 cups cold unsweetened grape juice
Ice cubes
6 thin lemon slices

In a blender container, combine ginger ale, undrained pineapple, and Splenda. Cover and process on BLEND for 30 seconds or until mixture is smooth. Pour mixture into a pitcher. Add grape juice. Mix well to combine. Refrigerate for at least 30 minutes. Mix well again before serving. When serving, pour into tall glasses filled with ice cubes and garnish each glass with 1 lemon slice.

Each serving equals:

HE: 1 Fruit • 4 Optional Calories

64 Calories • 0 gm Fat • 0 gm Protein •
16 gm Carbohydrate • 8 mg Sodium •
13 mg Calcium • 0 gm Fiber

DIABETIC EXCHANGES: 1 Fruit

Party 'til the Cows Come Home
Buffet for Six (Or Even Twelve)

Sometimes you don't want the fuss of a sit-down dinner for a large group, but you still want to entertain. The solution: a big, beautiful, bountiful buffet! You get a chance to show off your stuff as a chef by offering some splendid salads and side dishes, a couple of exquisite entrées, and of course a couple of dazzling desserts. I've chosen these recipes because they do well in a buffet setup. They don't lose their charm after a half hour of sitting around, however, make sure you don't leave anything sitting in direct sunlight. Now, there's enough food here to feed up to twelve people, but it's a great meal for six with plenty of variety—and plenty of leftovers for your future use!

THE PLAN: You may not agree, but I'm calling this **The Creamiest Slaw.** I've created dozens of them, but this wins that award in my estimation. Make it a few hours or even a day ahead, along with **Pasta Buffet Salad** and **Apple Pecan Party Salad.** Just don't forget to stir everything right before you serve it! Now, both desserts are delightful made just before the party or the day before. **Majestic Banana Sour Cream Pie** is one of my most luscious desserts ever, but I bet Cliff will go running for my **Chocolate Raisin Spice Cake.** What's left? Three dishes that each require about a hour in the oven. I'd make the **Company Meat Loaf** first; it just gets better when it sets awhile. Then you can fix the creamy, cheesy **Buffet Line Potatoes** and scrumptious **Company Baked Chicken.** No one is going home hungry—you can be sure of that!

The Creamiest Slaw

⊙ Serves 6 (½ cup)

½ cup Kraft fat-free mayonnaise
2 tablespoons Land O Lakes no-fat sour cream
2 tablespoons apple cider vinegar
2 tablespoons Splenda Granular
1 tablespoon dried onion flakes
1 teaspoon dried parsley flakes
3 cups purchased coleslaw mix

In a large bowl, combine mayonnaise, sour cream, vinegar, Splenda, onion flakes, and parsley flakes. Add coleslaw mix. Mix well to combine. Cover and refrigerate for at least 30 minutes. Gently stir again just before serving.

HINT: 2½ cups shredded cabbage and ½ cup shredded carrots may be used in place of purchased coleslaw mix.

Each serving equals:

HE: ½ Vegetable • ¼ Slider

36 Calories • 0 gm Fat • 1 gm Protein •
8 gm Carbohydrate • 190 mg Sodium •
29 mg Calcium • 1 gm Fiber

DIABETIC EXCHANGES: ½ Vegetable •
½ Other Carbohydrate

Pasta Buffet Salad

● Serves 6 (½ cup)

½ cup Kraft fat-free mayonnaise
2 tablespoons sweet pickle relish
2 cups cold cooked rotini pasta, rinsed and drained
1 cup finely chopped celery
½ cup chopped onion
1 hard-boiled egg, chopped

In a large bowl, combine mayonnaise and pickle relish. Add rotini pasta, celery, and onion. Mix well to combine. Fold in chopped egg. Cover and refrigerate for at least 30 minutes. Gently stir again just before serving.

HINT: Usually 1½ cups uncooked rotini pasta cooks to about 2 cups.

Each serving equals:

HE: ⅔ Bread • ½ Vegetable • ¼ Slider •
8 Optional Calories

---

105 Calories • 1 gm Fat • 4 gm Protein •
20 gm Carbohydrate • 203 mg Sodium •
20 mg Calcium • 1 gm Fiber

DIABETIC EXCHANGES: 1 Starch • ½ Vegetable

Apple Pecan Party Salad

○ Serves 6 (½ cup)

½ cup Kraft fat-free mayonnaise

2 tablespoons Splenda Granular

2 teaspoons lemon juice

3 cups (6 small) cored, unpeeled, and diced
    Red Delicious apples

1½ cups chopped celery

3 tablespoons chopped pecans

In a large bowl, combine mayonnaise, Splenda, and lemon juice. Add apples and celery. Mix well to combine. Fold in pecans. Cover and refrigerate for at least 15 minutes. Gently stir again just before serving.

Each serving equals:

HE: 1 Fruit • ½ Fat • ½ Vegetable •
15 Optional Calories

79 Calories • 3 gm Fat • 0 gm Protein •
13 gm Carbohydrate • 179 mg Sodium •
18 mg Calcium • 2 gm Fiber

DIABETIC EXCHANGES: 1 Fruit • ½ Fat • ½ Vegetable

Buffet Line Potatoes

○ Serves 6

1 (10¾-ounce) can Healthy Request Cream of Mushroom
    Soup
¼ cup Land O Lakes no-fat sour cream
1½ cups shredded Kraft reduced-fat Cheddar cheese
¾ cup finely chopped onion
2 teaspoons dried parsley flakes
⅛ teaspoon black pepper
9 cups shredded loose-packed frozen potatoes

Preheat oven to 350 degrees. Spray an 8-by-12-inch baking dish with butter-flavored cooking spray. In a large bowl, combine mushroom soup and sour cream. Stir in Cheddar cheese, onion, parsley flakes, and black pepper. Add potatoes. Mix well to combine. Evenly spread mixture into prepared baking dish. Bake for 55 to 60 minutes. Place baking dish on a wire rack and let set for 5 minutes. Divide into 6 servings.

HINT: Mr. Dell's frozen shredded potatoes are a good choice, or raw shredded potatoes, rinsed and patted dry, may be used in place of frozen potatoes.

Each serving equals:

HE: 1¼ Protein • 1 Bread • ¼ Vegetable • ¼ Slider •
17 Optional Calories

193 Calories • 5 gm Fat • 11 gm Protein •
26 gm Carbohydrate • 408 mg Sodium •
258 mg Calcium • 2 gm Fiber

DIABETIC EXCHANGES: 1½ Starch • 1 Meat

Company Meat Loaf

❂ Serves 6

16 ounces extra-lean ground sirloin beef or turkey breast
½ cup + 1 tablespoon dried fine bread crumbs
1 cup chopped onion
1 (8-ounce) can Hunt's Tomato Sauce☆
⅛ teaspoon black pepper
¼ cup Splenda Granular
1 teaspoon prepared yellow mustard
1 tablespoon finely chopped fresh parsley or 1 teaspoon
    dried parsley flakes

Preheat oven to 350 degrees. Spray a 9-by-5-inch loaf pan with butter-flavored cooking spray. In a large bowl, combine meat, bread crumbs, onion, ¼ cup tomato sauce, and black pepper. Mix well to combine. Pat mixture into prepared loaf pan. Bake for 30 minutes. In a small bowl, combine remaining ¾ cup tomato sauce, Splenda, mustard, and parsley. Spoon sauce mixture evenly over partially baked meat loaf. Continue baking for 25 to 30 minutes. Place loaf pan on a wire rack and let set for 5 minutes. Divide into 6 servings.

Each serving equals:

HE: 2 Protein • 1 Vegetable • ½ Bread •
4 Optional Calories

156 Calories • 4 gm Fat • 17 gm Protein •
13 gm Carbohydrate • 358 mg Sodium •
36 mg Calcium • 1 gm Fiber

DIABETIC EXCHANGES: 2 Meat • 1 Vegetable • ½ Starch

Company Baked Chicken

● Serves 6

6 tablespoons all-purpose flour
24 ounces skinned and boned uncooked chicken breast,
cut into 6 pieces
1 (10¾-ounce) can Healthy Request Cream of Chicken Soup
¼ cup Land O Lakes Fat Free Half & Half
1½ teaspoons dried onion flakes
1½ teaspoons dried parsley flakes
⅛ teaspoon black pepper

Preheat oven to 350 degrees. Spray an 8-by-12-inch baking dish with butter-flavored cooking spray. Place flour in a shallow dish. Coat chicken pieces on both sides in flour. Evenly arrange coated chicken in prepared baking dish. In a medium bowl, combine chicken soup, half & half, onion flakes, parsley flakes, black pepper, and any remaining flour. Spoon soup mixture evenly over chicken pieces. Cover and bake for 45 minutes. Uncover and continue baking for 15 minutes or until chicken is fork-tender. Place baking dish on a wire rack and let set for at least 5 minutes. When serving, evenly spoon sauce mixture over chicken pieces.

Each serving equals:

HE: 3 Protein • ⅓ Bread • ¼ Slider •
10 Optional Calories

184 Calories • 4 gm Fat • 25 gm Protein •
12 gm Carbohydrate • 261 mg Sodium •
30 mg Calcium • 0 gm Fiber

DIABETIC EXCHANGES: 3 Meat • ½ Starch •
½ Other Carbohydrate

Chocolate Raisin Spice Cake

● Serves 8

1 cup hot water

1 cup seedless raisins

1 cup Splenda Granular

1½ cups Bisquick Reduced Fat Baking Mix

¼ cup unsweetened cocoa powder

¼ teaspoon ground cinnamon

1 egg or equivalent in egg substitute

¾ cup Kraft fat-free mayonnaise

¼ cup chopped walnuts

½ cup Cool Whip Lite

Preheat oven to 350 degrees. Spray a 9-by-9-inch cake pan with butter-flavored cooking spray. In a medium bowl, combine hot water and raisins. Let set for 15 minutes. Stir Splenda into cooled raisin mixture. In a large bowl, combine baking mix, cocoa powder, and cinnamon. Add raisin mixture, egg, and mayonnaise. Mix well to combine. Fold in walnuts. Spread batter into prepared cake pan. Bake for 28 to 32 minutes or until a toothpick inserted in center comes out clean. Place cake pan on a wire rack and let set for at least 15 minutes. Cut into 8 servings. When serving, top each piece with 1 tablespoon Cool Whip Lite.

Each serving equals:

HE: 1 Bread • 1 Fruit • ¼ Protein • ¼ Fat • ¼ Slider • 9 Optional Calories

---

205 Calories • 5 gm Fat • 4 gm Protein • 36 gm Carbohydrate • 427 mg Sodium • 42 mg Calcium • 2 gm Fiber

---

DIABETIC EXCHANGES: 1 Starch • 1 Fruit • ½ Fat • ½ Other Carbohydrate

Majestic Banana Sour Cream Pie

○ Serves 8

> 2 (4-serving) packages JELL-O sugar-free instant
>   banana cream pudding mix
> 1⅓ cups Carnation Nonfat Dry Milk Powder
> 2¼ cups water
> ½ cup Land O Lakes no-fat sour cream
> 1 (6-ounce) Keebler graham cracker piecrust
> 2 cups (2 medium) sliced bananas
> ¾ cup Cool Whip Free
> ½ teaspoon coconut extract
> 2 tablespoons purchased graham cracker crumbs or
>   2 (2½-inch) graham cracker squares made into crumbs
> 2 tablespoons flaked coconut

In a large bowl, combine dry pudding mixes, dry milk powder, and water. Mix well using a wire whisk. Blend in sour cream. Evenly spread about ½ cup pudding mixture in bottom of piecrust. Arrange banana slices evenly over top. Spread remaining pudding mixture evenly over bananas. Refrigerate for 5 minutes. In a small bowl, gently combine Cool Whip Free and coconut extract. Drop by tablespoonful onto set filling to form 8 mounds. In a small bowl, combine graham cracker crumbs and coconut. Evenly sprinkle crumb mixture over top. Refrigerate for at least 1 hour. Cut into 8 servings.

HINTS: 1. To prevent bananas from turning brown, mix with 1 teaspoon lemon juice or sprinkle with Fruit Fresh.
2. A self-seal sandwich bag works great for crushing graham crackers.

Each serving equals:

HE: 1 Bread • ½ Fat Free Milk • ½ Fruit • ½ Fat •
¾ Slider • 1 Optional Calorie

230 Calories • 6 gm Fat • 6 gm Protein •
38 gm Carbohydrate • 493 mg Sodium •
174 mg Calcium • 1 gm Fiber

DIABETIC EXCHANGES: 1 Starch • 1 Fat •
½ Fat Free Milk • ½ Fruit • ½ Other Carbohydrate

"The Gang's All Here!"
Buffet for Eight

Want to invite a slightly bigger group for supper? Maybe you've got a two-table bridge party group that's due for a little celebration. Or perhaps you want to celebrate your hot-off-the-press master's degree in education! You already know I'm a fan of increasing your joy by sharing it with others, so this buffet menu is perfect for lots of family occasions and evenings with friends.

THE PLAN: Do the salads first, hours or even a day before your guests arrive. Any visiting children will find **Jellied Fruit Dew Salad** totally irresistible, and the adults will surely love my savory **Mixed Vegetable Salad with Mustard Dressing**. The same goes for two outrageously yummy desserts. **Upside-Down Cherry Bread Pudding** is rosy-red and truly delectable, while **Party "Amaretto" Cheesecake** simply sizzles with almond flavor. Next, boil the potatoes you'll need for **Cream Cheese Potatoes**, which will bake for forty-five minutes. You can also prepare **Cheesy Carrot Bake** and bake it side by side. My **Chicken-Mushroom Bake** can be readied in advance, then baked right before party time. Stir up a pretty pitcher of **Buffet Pink "Champagne" Punch** just before your guests arrive, and you'll surely be named "Hostess with the Mostess!"

Mixed Vegetable Salad with Mustard Dressing

🔾 Serves 8 (½ cup)

½ cup Splenda Granular
1 tablespoon all-purpose flour
½ cup white distilled vinegar
1 tablespoon prepared yellow mustard
2 teaspoons dried parsley flakes
1 (15-ounce) can mixed vegetables, rinsed and drained
1 (15-ounce) can red kidney beans, rinsed and drained
¾ cup chopped celery
¼ cup chopped onion

In a small saucepan sprayed with butter-flavored cooking spray, combine Splenda, flour, vinegar, mustard, and parsley flakes, using a wire whisk. Cook over medium heat for 5 minutes or until mixture thickens, stirring constantly. Remove from heat and let set 10 minutes. In a large bowl, combine mixed vegetables, kidney beans, celery, and onion. Add slightly cooled mustard dressing. Mix well to combine. Cover and refrigerate for at least 2 hours. Gently stir again just before serving.

Each serving equals:

HE: ½ Protein • ½ Vegetable • ¼ Bread •
10 Optional Calories

56 Calories • 0 gm Fat • 3 gm Protein •
11 gm Carbohydrate • 159 mg Sodium •
25 mg Calcium • 2 gm Fiber

DIABETIC EXCHANGES: ½ Vegetable • ½ Starch

Jellied Fruit Dew Salad

◐ Serves 8

1 cup unsweetened orange juice
2 cups Diet Mountain Dew☆
2 (4-serving) packages JELL-O sugar-free orange gelatin
1 (8-ounce) can pineapple tidbits, packed in fruit juice, drained
1 (11-ounce) can mandarin oranges, rinsed and drained
1 cup (1 medium) diced banana

In a medium saucepan, combine orange juice and 1 cup Diet Mountain Dew. Bring mixture to a boil, stirring often. Remove from heat. Add dry gelatin. Mix well to dissolve gelatin. Stir in remaining 1 cup Diet Mountain Dew. Add pineapple, mandarin oranges, and banana. Mix well to combine. Carefully pour mixture into an 8-by-8-inch dish. Refrigerate until firm, about 3 hours. Cut into 8 servings.

HINT: To prevent banana from turning brown, mix with 1 teaspoon lemon juice or sprinkle with Fruit Fresh.

Each serving equals:

HE: ¾ Fruit • 10 Optional Calories

---

60 Calories • 0 gm Fat • 1 gm Protein •
14 gm Carbohydrate • 40 mg Sodium •
8 mg Calcium • 1 gm Fiber

DIABETIC EXCHANGES: 1 Fruit

Cheesy Carrot Bake

● Serves 8

3½ cups frozen sliced carrots, thawed

½ cup finely chopped onion

1 (10¾-ounce) can Healthy Request Cream of Chicken Soup

¼ cup fat-free milk

¾ cup shredded Kraft reduced-fat Cheddar cheese

1 teaspoon dried parsley flakes

⅛ teaspoon black pepper

10 Ritz Reduced Fat Crackers, made into fine crumbs

Preheat oven to 350 degrees. Spray an 8-by-8-inch baking dish with butter-flavored cooking spray. Evenly arrange carrots in prepared baking dish. Sprinkle onion evenly over carrots. In a medium bowl, combine chicken soup, milk, Cheddar cheese, parsley flakes, and black pepper. Spoon soup mixture evenly over carrots. Evenly sprinkle cracker crumbs over top. Lightly spray crumbs with butter-flavored cooking spray. Bake for 30 to 35 minutes. Place baking dish on a wire rack and let set 5 minutes. Divide into 8 servings.

HINTS: 1. Thaw carrots by placing in a colander and rinsing under hot water for 1 minute.
2. 2 (15-ounce) cans sliced carrots, rinsed and drained can be used in place of frozen carrots.
3. A self-seal sandwich bag works great for crushing crackers.

Each serving equals:

HE: 1 Vegetable • ½ Protein • ¼ Bread • ¼ Slider • 2 Optional Calories

91 Calories • 3 gm Fat • 4 gm Protein • 12 gm Carbohydrate • 278 mg Sodium • 96 mg Calcium • 2 gm Fiber

DIABETIC EXCHANGES: 1 Vegetable • ½ Meat • ½ Other Carbohydrate

Cream Cheese Potatoes

○ Serves 8

6 cups peeled and diced raw potatoes
3 cups water
1 (8-ounce) package Philadelphia fat-free cream cheese
1 tablespoon Land O Lakes Fat Free Half & Half
1 egg, slightly beaten, or equivalent in egg substitute
1 (2-ounce) jar chopped pimiento, drained
2 tablespoons chopped fresh parsley or 2 teaspoons
    dried parsley flakes
⅛ teaspoon black pepper

Preheat oven to 350 degrees. Spray an 8-by-12-inch baking dish with butter-flavored cooking spray. In a large saucepan, combine potatoes and water. Bring to a boil. Cook over medium heat for 10 to 15 minutes or until potatoes are tender. Drain well. Mash potatoes with potato masher or electric mixer. Add cream cheese, half & half, egg, pimiento, parsley, and black pepper. Mix well to combine, until potatoes are light and fluffy. Evenly spread mixture into prepared baking dish. Bake for 45 minutes or until top is lightly browned. Place baking dish on a wire rack and let set for 5 minutes. Divide into 8 servings.

Each serving equals:

HE: ¾ Bread • ½ Protein • 8 Optional Calories

125 Calories • 1 gm Fat • 7 gm Protein •
22 gm Carbohydrate • 283 mg Sodium •
99 mg Calcium • 2 gm Fiber

DIABETIC EXCHANGES: 1 Starch • ½ Meat

Chicken-Mushroom Bake

○ Serves 8

32 ounces skinned and boned uncooked chicken breast,
    cut into 8 pieces
1 (10¾-ounce) can Healthy Request Cream of Chicken Soup
⅓ cup Land O Lakes Fat Free Half & Half
1 (4-ounce) can sliced mushrooms, drained
2 teaspoons dried onion flakes
1 teaspoon dried parsley flakes

Preheat oven to 350 degrees. Spray a 9-by-13-inch baking pan with butter-flavored cooking spray. Evenly arrange chicken pieces in prepared pan. In a medium bowl, combine chicken soup and half & half. Add mushrooms, onion flakes, and parsley flakes. Mix well to combine. Evenly spoon soup mixture over chicken pieces. Bake for 45 to 50 minutes or until chicken is tender.

Each serving equals:

HE: 3 Protein • ¼ Vegetable • ¼ Slider •
11 Optional Calories

156 Calories • 4 gm Fat • 24 gm Protein •
6 gm Carbohydrate • 284 mg Sodium •
30 mg Calcium • 1 gm Fiber

DIABETIC EXCHANGES: 3 Meat • ½ Other Carbohydrate

Upside-Down Cherry Bread Pudding

● Serves 8

8 slices reduced-calorie white bread, torn into small pieces
1 (4-serving) package JELL-O sugar-free vanilla cook-and-serve
  pudding mix
⅔ cup Carnation Nonfat Dry Milk Powder
2 cups water
1 teaspoon vanilla extract
2 (20-ounce) cans Lucky Leaf No Sugar Added Cherry Pie Filling

Preheat oven to 350 degrees. Spray an 8-by-12-inch baking dish with butter-flavored cooking spray. Evenly arrange bread pieces in prepared baking dish. In a large bowl, combine dry pudding mix, dry milk powder, water, and vanilla extract. Carefully pour pudding mixture evenly over bread. If any bread pieces are not covered by pudding mixture, push them down into mixture. Evenly spoon cherry pie filling over top. Bake for 45 to 50 minutes. Place baking dish on a wire rack and let set for 5 minutes. Divide into 8 servings.

HINT: Good warm or cold.

Each serving equals:

HE: 1 Fruit • ½ Bread • ¼ Fat Free Milk •
10 Optional Calories

101 Calories • 1 gm Fat • 4 gm Protein •
19 gm Carbohydrate • 212 mg Sodium •
92 mg Calcium • 1 gm Fiber

DIABETIC EXCHANGES: 1 Fruit • ½ Starch •
½ Other Carbohydrate

Party "Amaretto" Cheesecake

◐ Serves 8

2 (8-ounce) packages
  Philadelphia fat-free
  cream cheese
1 (4-serving) package JELL-O
  sugar-free instant vanilla
  pudding mix
⅔ cup Carnation Nonfat Dry
  Milk Powder
1 cup water

¼ cup Cool Whip Free
1 teaspoon almond extract
½ teaspoon coconut extract
1 (6-ounce) Keebler shortbread
  piecrust
¼ cup sliced almonds, toasted
2 tablespoons flaked coconut,
  toasted

In a large bowl, stir cream cheese with a sturdy spoon until
soft. Add dry pudding mix, dry milk powder, and water. Mix well
using a wire whisk. Gently blend in Cool Whip Free, almond
extract, and coconut extract. Spread mixture evenly into pie crust.
Sprinkle almonds and coconut evenly over top. Refrigerate for at
least 1 hour. Cut into 8 servings.

HINT: Toast almonds and coconut in a small skillet sprayed with
  butter-flavored cooking spray, stirring constantly for 1 to 2
  minutes. Remove skillet from heat and allow to cool completely before sprinkling over top of cheesecake.

Each serving equals:

HE: 1¼ Protein • 1 Bread • 1 Fat • ¼ Fat Free Milk •
1 Slider • 2 Optional Calories

---

240 Calories • 8 gm Fat • 13 gm Protein •
28 gm Carbohydrate • 523 mg Sodium •
252 mg Calcium • 1 gm Fiber

DIABETIC EXCHANGES: 1 Meat • 1 Starch • 1 Fat •
1 Other Carbohydrate

Buffet Pink "Champagne" Punch

○ Serves 8 (1 cup)

4 cups cold Diet 7-UP
4 cups cold water
1 tub Crystal Light Pink Lemonade mix

In a large pitcher, combine Diet 7-UP and water. Add dry lemonade mix. Mix well until dissolved, using a long-handled spoon. Serve at once or refrigerate until ready to serve.

Each serving equals:

HE: 4 Optional Calories

---

4 Calories • 0 gm Fat • 0 gm Protein •
1 gm Carbohydrate • 18 mg Sodium •
0 gm Calcium • 0 gm Fiber

DIABETIC EXCHANGES: Free Food

A "Welcome to the Neighborhood!" Party for Four

Has everyone on your block lived there forever? Or do you find yourself welcoming new neighbors every six months or so? The statistics say that Americans are on the move, which means many of us will need to throw a little 'do to welcome new neighbors to your town and street. This is also a great menu for an evening shared by two couples, or four buddies who haven't seen each other in a while. Invite a few girlfriends for a Russell Crowe film festival and sleepover—how many years has it been since you did *that*?

THE PLAN: For anyone who's convinced that it's not a party without chocolate, I give you a decadent **Chocolate Cheesecake with Cordial Cherry Topping**—utterly out of this world, and a definite make-ahead dish. You can also make my **Welcome! Veggie Dip** and cut up veggies to go with it in advance; just refrigerate and keep the veggies in cold water. Same goes for **Broccoli-Cauliflower Salad**, which overflows with enough crunch to spark any party. Your entrée, **Superb Baked Chicken**, takes an hour in the oven, and your **Baked Potatoes au Gratin** needs just a little less. **Party Peas and Carrots** is the last to do, taking only seven minutes on the stovetop. Make it memorable, make it fun, make it soon!

Welcome! Veggie Dip

❍ Serves 4 (3 tablespoons)

¼ cup Kraft fat-free mayonnaise
¼ cup Land O Lakes no-fat sour cream
¼ cup Kraft Fat Free Catalina Dressing
1 teaspoon prepared horseradish sauce
1 teaspoon Worcestershire sauce
2 tablespoons dried vegetable flakes
Celery sticks
Carrot sticks
Radishes

In a medium bowl, combine mayonnaise and sour cream. Add Catalina dressing, horseradish sauce, Worcestershire sauce, and dried vegetable flakes. Mix well to combine. Spoon mixture into an attractive dipping bowl and arrange dip and vegetables on serving plate.

Each serving equals:

HE: ½ Slider • 4 Optional Calories

44 Calories • 0 gm Fat • 1 gm Protein •
10 gm Carbohydrate • 305 mg Sodium •
27 mg Calcium • 0 gm Fiber

DIABETIC EXCHANGES: ½ Other Carbohydrate

Broccoli-Cauliflower Salad

○ Serves 4 (¾ cup)

1 cup chopped fresh broccoli
1 cup chopped fresh cauliflower
¼ cup chopped red onion
¼ cup seedless raisins
¼ cup chopped cashews
2 tablespoons Oscar Mayer or Hormel Real Bacon Bits
⅓ cup Kraft fat-free mayonnaise
1 tablespoon Land O Lakes Fat Free Half & Half
1 tablespoon Splenda Granular
1 tablespoon white distilled vinegar

In a large bowl, combine broccoli, cauliflower, onion, raisins, cashews, and bacon bits. In a small bowl, combine mayonnaise, half & half, Splenda, and vinegar. Add dressing mixture to broccoli mixture. Mix gently to combine. Cover and refrigerate for at least 15 minutes. Gently stir again just before serving.

Each serving equals:

HE: 1 Vegetable • ½ Fruit • ½ Fat • ¼ Protein • ¼ Slider • 9 Optional Calories

116 Calories • 4 gm Fat • 4 gm Protein • 16 gm Carbohydrate • 307 mg Sodium • 31 mg Calcium • 2 gm Fiber

DIABETIC EXCHANGES: 1 Vegetable • ½ Fruit • ½ Fat • ½ Other Carbohydrate

Party Peas and Carrots

○ Serves 4 (½ cup)

1 tablespoon apricot spreadable fruit

1 tablespoon + 1 teaspoon I Can't Believe It's Not Butter!
    Light Margarine

1 teaspoon dried onion flakes

1 teaspoon dried parsley flakes

⅛ teaspoon black pepper

3 cups frozen peas and carrots, thawed

In a medium saucepan sprayed with butter-flavored cooking spray, combine spreadable fruit, margarine, onion flakes, parsley flakes, and black pepper. Cook over medium heat for 2 minutes. Add peas and carrots. Mix well to combine. Continue cooking for 5 minutes or until mixture is heated through, stirring often.

HINT: Thaw peas and carrots by placing in a colander and rinsing under hot water for 1 minute.

Each serving equals:

HE: ½ Bread • ½ Fat • ½ Vegetable • ¼ Fruit

66 Calories • 2 gm Fat • 2 gm Protein •
10 gm Carbohydrate • 101 mg Sodium •
21 mg Calcium • 2 gm Fiber

DIABETIC EXCHANGES: ½ Starch • ½ Fat •
½ Vegetable

Baked Potatoes au Gratin

○ Serves 4

2½ cups thinly sliced cooked potatoes
1 cup + 2 tablespoons shredded Kraft reduced-fat
    Cheddar cheese
1 cup fat-free milk
¼ cup Land O Lakes Fat Free Half & Half
3 tablespoons all-purpose flour
1 tablespoon dried onion flakes
1 teaspoon dried parsley flakes
⅛ teaspoon black pepper

Preheat oven to 350 degrees. Spray an 8-by-8-inch baking dish with butter-flavored cooking spray. Evenly arrange potatoes in prepared baking dish. Sprinkle Cheddar cheese over potatoes. In a covered jar, combine milk, half & half, flour, onion flakes, parsley flakes, and black pepper. Shake well to blend. Pour milk mixture evenly over cheese. Cover and bake for 30 minutes. Uncover and continue baking for 15 minutes. Place baking dish on a wire rack and let set for 5 minutes. Divide into 4 servings.

Each serving equals:

HE: 1½ Protein • 1 Bread • ¼ Fat Free Milk • ¼ Slider • 11 Optional Calories

221 Calories • 5 gm Fat • 14 gm Protein • 30 gm Carbohydrate • 301 mg Sodium • 320 mg Calcium • 2 gm Fiber

DIABETIC EXCHANGES: 1½ Meat • 1½ Starch

Superb Baked Chicken

⚫ Serves 4

6 tablespoons Kraft fat-free mayonnaise
2 tablespoons Kraft Fat Free French Dressing
1 teaspoon dried onion flakes
2 teaspoons dried parsley flakes
⅛ teaspoon black pepper
16 ounces skinned and boned uncooked chicken breast,
*   cut into 4 pieces*
15 Ritz Reduced Fat Crackers, made into fine crumbs

Preheat oven to 350 degrees. Spray an 8-by-8-inch baking dish with butter-flavored cooking spray. In a medium bowl, combine mayonnaise, French dressing, onion flakes, parsley flakes, and black pepper. Coat chicken pieces in mayonnaise mixture, then roll in cracker crumbs. Evenly arrange chicken pieces in prepared baking dish. Drizzle any remaining dressing mixture and cracker crumbs over top of chicken pieces. Bake for 50 to 55 minutes or until chicken is thoroughly cooked. Place baking dish on a wire rack and let set for 5 minutes.

Each serving equals:

HE: 3 Protein • ¾ Bread • ¼ Slider •
6 Optional Calories

203 Calories • 3 gm Fat • 24 gm Protein •
20 gm Carbohydrate • 405 mg Sodium •
13 mg Calcium • 0 gm Fiber

DIABETIC EXCHANGES: 3 Meat • 1 Starch

Chocolate Cheesecake with Cordial Cherry Topping

○ Serves 8

2 (8-ounce) packages
   Philadelphia fat-free
   cream cheese
1 (4-serving) package JELL-O
   sugar-free instant white
   chocolate pudding mix
⅔ cup Carnation Nonfat Dry
   Milk Powder
1 cup water

1 cup Cool Whip Free☆
1 (6-ounce) Keebler chocolate
   pie crust
½ teaspoon brandy extract
5 to 6 drops red food coloring
8 maraschino cherries☆
2 tablespoons mini chocolate
   chips

In a large bowl, stir cream cheese with a sturdy spoon until soft. Add dry pudding mix, dry milk powder, and water. Mix well using a wire whisk. Fold in ¼ cup Cool Whip Free. Spread mixture into piecrust. Refrigerate while preparing topping. In a small bowl, combine remaining ¾ cup Cool Whip Free, brandy extract, and red food coloring. Chop 4 maraschino cherries into small pieces. Gently fold into topping mixture. Spread topping mixture evenly over set filling and sprinkle chocolate chips evenly over top. Cut remaining 4 maraschino cherries in half. Garnish top with cherry halves. Refrigerate for at least 1 hour. Cut into 8 servings.

Each serving equals:

HE: 1 Bread • 1 Protein • ¼ Fat Free Milk • ¼ Fat •
½ Slider • 10 Optional Calories

217 Calories • 5 gm Fat • 11 gm Protein •
32 gm Carbohydrate • 541 mg Sodium •
235 mg Calcium • 1 gm Fiber

DIABETIC EXCHANGES: 1 Starch • 1 Meat • ½ Fat •
1 Other Carbohydrate

A Culinary Celebration for Eight

Cooking for a crowd can be a lot of work, but here's one of my favorite celebration meals, carefully designed (by me!) to make it easier on the chef. Most cooks struggle to juggle their menu items so that everything either needs to be stirred on the stovetop or squeezed into the oven simultaneously. These days, many kitchens boast a double oven plus a microwave, but if you've got a smaller setup, don't despair. Most of my recipes reheat beautifully, so make a couple of dishes earlier and warm them while others are setting up.

THE PLAN: I like using a decorative dish for the **Green Garden Relish Mold,** so if you've got something pretty handed down from a relative, use it! Make it in the morning so it has plenty of time to jell. You also want to fill your slow cooker for the **Olive Beef Roast** early in the day, so it has time to get wonderfully tender and flavorful. With these dishes, you'll be serving **Mashed Potato Bake** (allow about ten minutes for prep and twenty minutes in the oven) and **Green Beans Almondine** (ten to twelve minutes on top of the stove). Toast your loved ones with **Party "Champagne" Punch** and send them home happy with my delectable **Cardinal Sundaes.** If it's late, leave the dishes for the morning. If not, invite your spouse or friend to chat while you finish up in the kitchen. Talking about a party is almost as much fun as having one!

Green Garden Relish Mold

◑ Serves 8

1 (4-serving) package JELL-O sugar-free lime gelatin
1 cup boiling water
¾ cup cold water
1 tablespoon white distilled vinegar
½ cup finely chopped peeled cucumber
1 cup finely sliced celery
1 cup finely shredded cabbage
¼ cup finely sliced green onion
8 lettuce leaves
½ cup Land O Lakes no-fat sour cream

In a large bowl, combine dry gelatin and boiling water. Mix well to dissolve gelatin. Stir in cold water and vinegar. Add cucumber, celery, cabbage, and onion. Pour mixture into an 8-by-8-inch dish. Refrigerate until firm, about 3 hours. Cut into 8 servings. When serving, place a lettuce leaf on a salad plate, arrange salad on lettuce and top each with 1 tablespoon sour cream.

Each serving equals:

HE: ½ Vegetable • ¼ Slider

24 Calories • 0 gm Fat • 1 gm Protein •
5 gm Carbohydrate • 38 mg Sodium •
32 mg Calcium • 1 gm Fiber

DIABETIC EXCHANGES: ½ Vegetable

Green Beans Almondine

● Serves 8 (full ½ cup)

6 cups frozen French-style green beans, thawed
¼ cup water
¼ cup slivered almonds
1 tablespoon + 1 teaspoon I Can't Believe It's Not Butter!
*   Light Margarine*
2 tablespoons Land O Lakes Fat Free Half & Half
1½ teaspoons lemon pepper

In a large skillet sprayed with butter-flavored cooking spray, sauté green beans in water for 6 to 8 minutes. Add almonds, margarine, half & half, and lemon pepper. Mix well to combine. Lower heat and simmer for 3 to 4 minutes or until mixture is heated through, stirring occasionally.

Each serving equals:

HE: 1½ Vegetable • ½ Fat • 9 Optional Calories

79 Calories • 3 gm Fat • 3 gm Protein •
10 gm Carbohydrate • 89 mg Sodium •
72 mg Calcium • 3 gm Fiber

DIABETIC EXCHANGES: 1½ Vegetable • ½ Fat

Mashed Potato Bake

● Serves 8

2⅓ *cups instant potato flakes*

2¾ *cups boiling water*

1 *tablespoon* + 1 *teaspoon I Can't Believe It's Not Butter!*
    Light Margarine

1 *teaspoon prepared yellow mustard*

2 *teaspoons dried parsley flakes*

1 *teaspoon lemon pepper*

¾ *cup shredded Kraft reduced-fat Cheddar cheese*☆

¼ *cup crushed cornflakes*

Preheat oven to 325 degrees. Spray an 8-by-12-inch baking dish with butter-flavored cooking spray. In a large bowl, combine dry potato flakes and boiling water. Mix well with a fork until fluffy. Stir in margarine, mustard, parsley flakes, lemon pepper, and ½ cup Cheddar cheese. Evenly spread mixture into prepared baking dish. In a small bowl, combine crushed cornflakes and remaining ¼ cup Cheddar cheese. Evenly sprinkle mixture over potato mixture. Lightly spray top with butter-flavored cooking spray. Bake for 20 minutes. Place baking dish on a wire rack and let set for 5 minutes. Divide into 8 servings.

Each serving equals:

HE: 1 Bread • ½ Protein • ¼ Fat

---

87 Calories • 3 gm Fat • 4 gm Protein •
11 gm Carbohydrate • 203 mg Sodium •
72 mg Calcium • 1 gm Fiber

DIABETIC EXCHANGES: 1 Starch • ½ Meat • ½ Fat

Olive Beef Roast

● Serves 8

1 (3-pound) uncooked lean beef roast
1 (10¾-ounce) can Healthy Request Tomato Soup
½ cup sliced pimiento-stuffed green olives
1 cup chopped onion
⅛ teaspoon black pepper

Spray a slow cooker container with butter-flavored cooking spray. Place beef roast in prepared container. In a small bowl, combine tomato soup, olives, onion, and black pepper. Spoon soup mixture evenly over roast. Cover and cook on LOW for 6 to 8 hours. Remove roast and cut into 8 pieces. When serving, evenly spoon sauce mixture over meat.

Each serving equals:

HE: 4 Protein • ¼ Fat • ¼ Vegetable • ¼ Slider •
2 Optional Calories

---

221 Calories • 9 gm Fat • 28 gm Protein •
7 gm Carbohydrate • 302 mg Sodium •
14 mg Calcium • 1 gm Fiber

DIABETIC EXCHANGES: 4 Meat • ½ Other Carbohydrate

Cardinal Sundaes

O Serves 8

> 1 (4-serving) package JELL-O sugar-free raspberry gelatin
> 2 (4-serving) packages JELL-O sugar-free vanilla cook-and-serve
>   pudding mix
> 1 cup unsweetened orange juice
> 1 cup Diet Mountain Dew
> 3 cups frozen unsweetened red raspberries, partially thawed
> 4 cups Wells' Blue Bunny sugar- and fat-free vanilla ice cream or
>   any sugar- and fat-free ice cream

In a large saucepan, combine dry gelatin, dry pudding mixes, orange juice, and Diet Mountain Dew. Cook over medium heat until mixture thickens and starts to boil, stirring often. Add raspberries. Mix gently to combine. Remove from heat. Gently stir mixture again. For each serving, place ½ cup ice cream in a dessert dish and spoon about ½ cup warm raspberry mixture over top. Serve at once.

Each serving equals:

HE: ¾ Fruit • ½ Fat Free Milk • ½ Slider •
13 Optional Calories

128 Calories • 0 gm Fat • 4 gm Protein •
28 gm Carbohydrate • 113 mg Sodium •
132 mg Calcium • 3 gm Fiber

DIABETIC EXCHANGES: 1 Fruit • 1 Other Carbohydrate

Party "Champagne" Punch

○ Serves 8 (1 cup)

4 cups cold unsweetened apple juice
2 cups cold Diet Mountain Dew
2 cups cold club soda

In a large pitcher, combine apple juice, Diet Mountain Dew, and club soda. Pour into champagne glasses. Serve at once.

Each serving equals:

HE: 1 Fruit

---

56 Calories • 0 gm Fat • 0 gm Protein •
14 gm Carbohydrate • 9 mg Sodium •
8 mg Calcium • 0 gm Fiber

DIABETIC EXCHANGES: 1 Fruit

Index

Making Healthy Exchanges Work for You

You're ready now to begin a wonderful journey to better health. In the preceding pages, you've discovered the remarkable variety of good food available to you when you begin eating the Healthy Exchanges way. You've stocked your pantry and learned many of my food preparation "secrets" that will point you on the way to delicious success.

But before I let you go, I'd like to share a few tips that I've learned while traveling toward healthier eating habits. It took me a long time to learn how to eat *smarter*. In fact, I'm still working on it. But I am getting better. For years, I could *inhale* a five-course meal in five minutes flat—and still make room for a second helping of dessert!

Now I follow certain signposts on the road that help me stay on the right path. I hope these ideas will help point you in the right direction as well.

1. **Eat slowly** so your brain has time to catch up with your tummy. Cut and chew each bite slowly. Try putting your fork down between bites. Stop eating as soon as you feel full. Crumple your napkin and throw it on top of your plate so you don't continue to eat when you are no longer hungry.

2. **Smaller plates** may help you feel more satisfied by your food portions *and* limit the amount you can put on the plate.

3. **Watch portion size.** If you are *truly* hungry, you can always add more food to your plate once you've finished your initial serving. But remember to count the additional food accordingly.

4. **Always eat at your dining-room or kitchen table.** You deserve better than nibbling from an open refrigerator or over the sink. Make an attractive place setting, even if you're eating alone. Feed your eyes as well as your stomach. By always eating at a table, you will become much more aware of your true food intake. For some reason, many of us conveniently "forget" the food we swallow while standing over the stove or munching in the car or on the run.

5. **Avoid doing anything else while you are eating.** If you read the paper or watch television while you eat, it's easy to consume too much food without realizing it, because you are concentrating on something else besides what you're eating. Then, when you look down at your plate and see that it's empty, you wonder where all the food went and why you still feel hungry.

Day by day, as you travel the path to good health, it will become easier to make the right choices, to eat *smarter*. But don't ever fool yourself into thinking that you'll be able to put your eating habits on cruise control and forget about them. Making a commitment to eat good healthy food and sticking to it takes some effort. But with all the good-tasting recipes in this Healthy Exchanges cookbook, just think how well you're going to eat—and enjoy it—from now on!

Healthy Lean Bon Appétit!

I want to hear from you . . .

Besides my family, the love of my life is creating "common folk" healthy recipes and solving everyday cooking questions in *The Healthy Exchanges Way*. Everyone who uses my recipes is considered part of the Healthy Exchanges Family, so please write to me if you have any questions, comments, or suggestions. I will do my best to answer. With your support, I'll continue to stir up even more recipes and cooking tips for the Family in the years to come.

Write to: JoAnna M. Lund
c/o Healthy Exchanges, Inc.
P.O. Box 80
DeWitt, IA 52742-0080

If you prefer, you can fax me at 1-563-659-2126 or contact me via e-mail by writing to HealthyJo@aol.com. Or visit my Healthy Exchanges Internet website at: www.healthyexchanges.com.

Now That You've Seen the
Family & Friends Cookbook,
Why Not Order
The Healthy Exchanges Food Newsletter?

If you enjoyed the recipes in this cookbook and would like to cook up even more of these "common folk" healthy dishes, you may want to subscribe to *The Healthy Exchanges Food Newsletter*.

This monthly 12-page newsletter contains 30-plus new recipes *every month* in such columns as:

- Reader Exchange
- Reader Requests
- Recipe Makeover
- Micro Corner
- Dinner for Two

- Plug It In
- Meatless Main Dishes
- Rise & Shine
- Our Small World

- Brown Bagging It
- Snack Attack
- Side Dishes
- Main Dishes
- Desserts

In addition to all the recipes, other regular features include:

- The Editor's Motivational Corner
- Dining Out Question & Answer
- Cooking Question & Answer
- New Product Alert
- Success Profiles of Winners in the Losing Game
- Exercise Advice from a Cardiac Rehab Specialist
- Nutrition Advice from a Registered Dietitian
- Positive Thought for the Month

The cost for a one-year (12-issue) subscription is $25. To order, call our toll-free number and pay with any major credit card, or send a check to the address on page 319 of this book.

1-800-766-8961 for Customer Orders
1-563-659-8234 for Customer Service

Thank you for your order, and for choosing to become a part of the Healthy Exchanges Family!